SCHOOL VOUCHERS

EXAMINING THE EVIDENCE

Other books from the Economic Policy Institute

The State of Working America 2000-2001

The Class Size Policy Debate

Risky Business:
Private Management of Public Schools

Where's the Money Gone?
Changes in the Level and Composition of Education Spending

School Choice:
Examining the Evidence

SCHOOL VOUCHERS

EXAMINING THE EVIDENCE

By Martin Carnoy

ECONOMIC POLICY INSTITUTE

Washington, D.C.

Martin Carnoy, a professor of education and economics at Stanford University, has written extensively about education, labor markets, and the changing international economy. Some of his recent books include *The New Global Economy in the Information Age* (with M. Castells, S. Cohen, and F. H. Cardoso), *Decentralization and School Improvement* (with Jane Hannaway), *Faded Dreams: the Economics and Politics of Race in America,* and, most recently, *Sustainable Flexibility: Work, Family, and Community in the Information Age,* published by Harvard University Press and the Russell Sage Foundation. He is also the editor of the *International Encyclopedia of the Economics of Education*. Prof. Carnoy came to the School of Education at Stanford in 1969, where he helped build the International and Comparative Education Program.

Acknowledgments: I would like to thank Dominic Brewer, Brian Gill, Doug Harris, Larry Mishel, Bella Rosenberg, and Jennifer King Rice for their helpful comments and critiques of earlier drafts, and Tom Kane and Susanna Loeb for providing feedback at critical junctures. Obviously, the responsibility for the final product is mine.

ECONOMIC POLICY INSTITUTE
1660 L Street, NW, Suite 1200
Washington, D.C. 20036

http://www.epinet.org

ISBN: 0-944826-94-6

Table of contents

Executive summary

School vouchers have been in the limelight for a decade. The basic argument is that giving parents public funds to send their children to private schools will stimulate innovation and competition among schools. Although vouchers lack broad public support, parents in low-income inner cities are more likely to favor alternatives to traditional public education, and this interest has stimulated small pilot programs in a few urban school districts. Such programs have the potential to inform public debate about vouchers' strengths and weaknesses, but they have been evaluated mainly by researchers who openly and actively support vouchers. Yet the media tend to report results from these analyses without necessary caveats and alternative views. Now that the push for vouchers has reached the federal government through President Bush's education initiative, the urgency for a balanced perspective has become more important than ever.

Do school vouchers improve student performance? A review of the evidence finds that vouchers' effects on student achievement are almost certainly smaller than claimed by pro-voucher researchers. Although programs in many cities were designed to be like randomized-trial medical experiments—with high validity and reliability—common problems in implementation may have compromised validity and produced misleading results. Moreover, the results are marked by broad inconsistencies across grades, academic subjects, and racial groups.

Recent highly publicized research involving Florida schools also highlights the difficulty in attributing test score gains to vouchers, since many of these programs involve not only vouchers but also school grading systems and others variables at the same time. The same researchers who found large effects from earlier voucher programs also found large voucher effects in Florida. But a closer look reveals that most of the gains could have been caused by the school grading system, not vouchers. In three states with school grading systems—Texas, North Carolina, and Florida before vouchers—low-performing schools (sometimes referred to as "F" schools) produced gains quite similar to those of the Florida voucher program. Thus, the "scarlet letter" effect from identifying low-performing schools is as plausible an explanation for the test score gains as is the voucher threat.

Identifying the effects of programs is a challenging task, especially for vouchers. As the evidence slowly comes in, a balanced analysis suggests that voucher effects may exist, but they are significantly smaller than voucher proponents would have the public and the media believe.

Introduction

School vouchers have been in the limelight for almost a decade, mainly at the state and local level. But with George Bush's candidacy and his election to the presidency, they have now become a national issue. At the same time, voucher advocates have produced new reports claiming that students using vouchers improve their academic performance and that the threat of the availability of vouchers leads to improved student performance in public schools. The results of these reports have been widely—and largely uncritically—circulated in the press. They give the impression that vouchers are the solution to the educational woes of minority students in "failing" public schools. The problem is real, but do these studies support their claims? The empirical findings on the educational effects of vouchers deserve a closer look.

The idea of public funding of private schools is not new, nor does it belong exclusively to conservative free market reformers. In the 1960s and early 1970s, academics on the left, such as Christopher Jencks (1966), argued that vast differences between the quality of public schooling for inner-city blacks and suburban whites could not be resolved within the structure of a residentially segregated public education system. Jencks argued for a policy concept introduced by Milton Friedman (1955) more than a decade earlier. Friedman proposed to offer public funds to families that could be used only for education but in any educational institution, public or private. Such "vouchers" would serve to give families increased choice of the kind of education their children received. Friedman saw vouchers as a way to break the "monopoly" of the public sector over education and increase consumer choice, hence economic welfare. Jencks saw vouchers as a way of improving educational opportunities for a historically discriminated-against group within American society. Both shared a distrust of the state—Friedman of the bureau-centric state interfering with "democratic" markets, Jencks of the class/race-centric state reproducing inequality through public education. But conditions may have changed in the last 40 years. While there is still a glaring gap between achievement of black and white students, the gap has been considerably narrowed. In the last decade the progress seems to have stopped, but it is unclear what the causes of the continued gap might be.[1] The voucher issue therefore has two different political origins. One is a conservative, free market ideology that prefers private to public provision of any services, and the second is the practical demand of low-income parents for better schooling, public or private. Even if private schools were no more effective than public schools, market reformers would insist that vouchers make parents and children better off because of choice and competition, and that private school choice should be made available to all parents, regardless of income. But the demand in inner cities for better schooling is based not on free market ideology but on academic results.

Whatever the origin of their support for vouchers, advocates have been attempting to support two claims: first, that private schools supported by public funds actually can do a better job than public schools of educating the children most at-risk of school failure, whether because vouchers are a route to smaller classes and better teachers, or because private schools are superior in other respects; and second, that vouchers increase incentives for public schools to improve by threatening low-performing public schools with the loss of students to competing private schools.

In the last few years, the leading proponent of the idea that private schools are demonstrably more effective at educating low-income African American students and an effective mechanism for improving public education has been Harvard Professor Paul Peterson. The research support for these claims is controversial, in large part because the Peterson group's statistical analysis seems always tilted to favor a positive result for vouchers. The history of such tilting is no longer just support generated for the alleged greater effectiveness of private education; it has also carried over into the claims regarding vouchers as a stimulus to better public schooling. In February 2001, Jay Greene, now a researcher at the Manhattan Institute, published a short paper assessing the impact of the Florida voucher plan on "failing" schools. All of these studies bear extremely close scrutiny.

This study reviews the recent empirical research in these two areas: (1) the effect of vouchers on student achievement, particularly for low-income minorities enabled to go to private schools; and (2) the effect of the threat of vouchers on low-performing public schools.

Among its findings:

- Research on the effect of vouchers in Milwaukee and Cleveland showed anywhere from no effects to small effects of vouchers for mainly African American students. Studies in Cleveland suggest that the achievement gains after two years in existing religious schools for voucher students were higher in one subject, science. Voucher students in for-profit private schools did significantly worse than non-voucher students in one study, but did better and then worse according to another. The much larger size of the voucher in Milwaukee (about $5,500 currently) than in Cleveland (maximum $2,500) also suggests that, whether test scores in private schools are higher or not, a larger voucher induces many more families to transfer their children to private schools and induces more private schools to offer educational services to low-income students.

- Research in Dayton, New York, and Washington (conducted and evaluated by voucher proponent Paul Peterson and his colleagues) show no significant test score gains for Hispanic and white voucher recipients, but it did find gains for African Americans that were statistically significant overall in New York and Washington and marginally significant in Dayton (in reading only). But several methodological issues make these comparisons of achievement gains problematic. These issues include the inability to ensure that participants are available for follow-up evaluation; the inability to explain differences in outcome by grade/age and ethnic cohort; inconsistent inclusion and exclusion of data on students who experience either large gains or large drops in test scores.

- Findings that the threat of vouchers for students in "failing" (F) public schools caused math and writing gains among Florida's lowest-performing schools to increase significantly more than the gains of higher-performing schools are plagued by methodological problems. The research tends to overestimate the effect of being designated an F school, and it offers no evidence that the higher estimated test-score gain by an F school should be attributed to the threat of vouchers.

Chapter 1

Do vouchers for private education raise student achievement?

In the most recent salvo in the voucher debate, Paul Peterson and his colleagues (William Howell of the University of Wisconsin, Patrick Wolf of Georgetown University, and David Campbell, also of Harvard (Howell et al. 2000)) announced in August 2000 that their voucher experiments in New York, Washington, D.C., and Dayton, Ohio showed that at least some pupils—African Americans—achieve better in private than in public schools. The finding was widely hailed by voucher supporters across the political spectrum as showing that private schools could solve a problem public schools apparently could not—the lagging achievement of low-income inner-city black children.

As Robert Reich wrote in the *Wall Street Journal* (Reich 2000), "[e]vidence mounts that vouchers do work for kids who use them. A new study of students in New York, Washington, and Dayton, Ohio—conducted by researchers at Harvard, Georgetown, and the University of Wisconsin—found that after two years, the average performance of black students who switched to private schools was 6% higher than that of students who stayed behind in public schools. So why not simply 'voucherize' all education funding and let students and their parents select where they can get the best education?" And, as William Safire commented in the *New York Times* (Safire 2000), "This hard evidence is not what teacher unionists want to hear....The Harvard study shows Bush is on the right side of this. He should embrace the successful voucher students and joyfully join the controversy...."

But soon after the results were presented, another member of the Peterson team, David Myers, contractor for the New York City part of the research, challenged Peterson's interpretation, arguing that the New York results—even for African American students—were not convincing enough to support the Peterson group's policy conclusions. Earlier voucher studies in Milwaukee and Cleveland seemed to support this more carefully worded view.

Who is right? Even if we thought that voucher proponents were willing to limit vouchers programs to low-income, inner-city families, how sanguine should we be that such inner-city (read African American) pupils would gain by switching to private schools?

The short answer is that the three-city study is not nearly as reliable as its authors claim. As a basis for educational policy, it should be interpreted cautiously. It is possible that a more structured private school environment with smaller classes and higher-achieving peers could help African Americans make greater gains than if they stayed in public schools. It is also possible that improvements to public schools would yield comparable improvements. But that said, the Peterson results may misrepresent gains that typical low-income African American students can make by switching to private schools. Using statistical techniques not easily understood by the media or the public, the studies' methodology is laced with potential biases. In the context of an intense ideological push for privatizing education, the question to ask is not *whether* these latest Peterson-group reports overestimate private school effects, but *by how much*.

In four cities—Dayton, New York, Washington, and Charlotte, N.C. (where data were released more recently)—the Peterson team built evaluations into the voucher plans themselves. Evaluating these evaluations is not easy, because, with the exception of New York, the researchers have not publicly released their data (the New York data were the most transparent because they were reported by grade). Earlier, though, in Milwaukee and Cleveland, the Peterson evaluations were constructed after the fact, and they included responses to research originally carried out by those not politically committed to vouchers. The Peterson estimates in those studies have a different character. For one, "experimental" controls were weaker or nonexistent. More important, the data were available to others and so were subject to re-analysis.

The Milwaukee voucher experiment

The longest-running voucher initiative in the U.S. is Milwaukee's. It began in 1991 on the initiative of Polly Williams, an African American Wisconsin legislator. The $2,500 vouchers were awarded by lottery to low-income families, 75% African Americans, to be used only in secular private schools. Schools had to accept the voucher as full payment (parents could not top it up). Initially, seven private schools agreed to take voucher students. Although the legislature set a maximum of 1,500 vouchers to be awarded, this number was never attained during the five years of the program. Enrollment increased steadily but slowly, from 341 in 1990-91 to 830 in 1994-95. The number of schools participating also increased, from seven in 1990-91 and six in 1991-92 to 11 in 1992-93 and 12 in 1994-5 and 1995-96.

The legislature commissioned University of Wisconsin professor John Witte and his colleagues to study the students who received vouchers and compare their achievement with similar students in public schools. Witte et al. found high levels of satisfaction among families receiving vouchers (Witte, Sterr, and Thorn 1995). Yet, when they analyzed achievement differences between those Milwaukee pupils who used vouchers to attend "choice schools" and Milwaukee public school pupils of similar socioeconomic background, race, and ethnicity, Witte et al. found that, generally, voucher students did no better in either math and reading. The one exception was a statistically significant *negative* effect of attending choice schools on reading scores in the second year of the program (1991-92). According to Witte et al., many of the poorest choice students left the program at the end of that second year. The authors also estimated the achievement effect controlling for the number of years the choice students had been in a private school. Again, private school voucher students did no better than public school students in either math or reading. The only effect that approached statistical significance was a negative reading score for those who had been in private schools for two years.

Witte et al. admitted that such an analysis has its limits, since many new students were being added to the private school sample every year, and a large fraction (about 30%) left the sample. The proportion leaving the sample was about the same for public school pupils. So the sample of private and public school pupils differed from year to year.

Other factors also changed in Milwaukee from year to year. The initial voucher was about one-half of Milwaukee's public school per-pupil spending. The voucher rose quickly, with private schools demanding and getting a higher voucher, until it was close to the primary school public cost per pupil when special education costs were accounted for. This is a major reason that more private schools were attracted into the program and more students could be accommodated in later years. Even so, over the course of the experiment, several of the participating private schools closed, including some due to bankruptcy.

In 1996 Peterson and his colleagues obtained the Milwaukee data and published their own study, using a "quasi-experimental" design that compared achievement of those who got vouchers in the lottery with those who did not. Peterson claimed that Witte had misspecified his model by comparing private school pupils with those who remained in public schools but had not necessarily applied for vouchers (Greene, Peterson, and Du 1996). In contrast, Greene et al. assumed that selection into the voucher program by lottery had resulted in a random sample of *applicants* being chosen to attend private schools. Thus, applicants should be the relevant pool from which to draw comparison groups. The results of their comparison showed pupils attending private schools making significant gains in both math and reading over the students who applied for vouchers but ended up attending public school. The gains were found in the third and fourth years of the voucher program.

Witte (1997) countered that students who applied but did not get vouchers included students who had gotten vouchers but were rejected by the private schools. In addition, many of those pupils who were in the "control group" (those who had applied for vouchers but not gotten them) could not be located to measure their later test scores as public school students. Some others who had originally applied for vouchers and did not get them attended private religious schools assisted by a parallel, privately funded choice program, Partners for Advancing Values in Education (PAVE), so were not included in the control group. Since these students were more likely to have more educated and motivated parents than those who stayed in public schools, the control group was not necessarily a random sample of those who did not get vouchers.[2]

A third party, Princeton economist Cecilia Rouse, then took the same data, reworked them and found that students in private schools made faster gains in math (after the second year), but none in reading (Rouse 1998a). The gains in math were statistically significant but relatively small. Rouse compared the choice students (those who had been selected to get a voucher, whether or not they had actually used it) with both Greene et al.'s comparison group and a sample of Milwaukee public school students, similar to that used by Witte et al. She corrected all three samples for an implicit set of student characteristics that are invariant over time (including but not limited to, native ability, race, ethnicity, socioeconomic background, as well as other, "unobservable," student attributes) but may be correlated with students' families applying to get vouchers. These are called student "fixed effects." She argues that her results disagree with Witte et al.'s because the latter restricted their samples to students for whom prior test scores were available (her fixed effects variable does not depend on measuring prior test scores) and disagree with Greene et al.'s because Greene et al.'s reading results disappear when student fixed effects are included. A second Rouse paper found that gains for low-income Milwaukee public school students in smaller classes were higher than the gains of voucher students in private schools, which also were characterized by much smaller class sizes than in Milwaukee public schools (Rouse 1998b).

In 1997 the Wisconsin legislature expanded the voucher program to 15,000 low-income students, and included religious schools. The legislation was upheld by the Wisconsin Supreme Court. Initially, about 8,000 students took up the vouchers, which continued to be worth about the cost of Milwaukee's per pupil spending on primary education ($5,500 in 1997). In the first year, about one-third of voucher takers under this expanded program were already in private schools but qualified because of their low family incomes. By the school year 2001-02, about 10,000 children will use vouchers at over 100 mostly religious private schools (Williams 2000).[3] This is a significant fraction of Milwaukee's 100,000 public school students. Even if only 7,500 of the voucher students were not already in private schools and transferred from public schools, the voucher program has shifted almost 8% of Milwaukee's public school students to private schools. This suggests that, given a large enough voucher, many low-income families will take advantage of it, and at least some new schools will come into the market. However, no one knows whether voucher students are performing better in this expanded program because, unlike public school students, they are not required by the legislature to take state tests, and no evaluation program is written into the legislation. We also know little about how many students who took up vouchers returned to public schools after a year or two in a private school.

The Cleveland voucher program

Cleveland's voucher program was approved by the Ohio legislature in June 1995 and began in the 1996-97 school year with a maximum voucher of $2,500. Voucher recipients were chosen by lottery and received a fixed percentage of tuition charged by private schools, the percentage depending on the family's income level. Students whose family income was at or above 200% of the poverty line received 75% of the school's tuition up to $2,500, and those below the poverty line received 90%, up to $2,500.

The Cleveland program differed from the Milwaukee experiment in several important aspects. In Cleveland, more than twice as many vouchers were offered as in Milwaukee (3,700 versus 1,500). Unlike Milwaukee families, Cleveland families had to add to the voucher to attend private schools, both because the voucher covered only part of tuition and because private schools could charge tuition higher than the voucher. As in Milwaukee, the program got off to a slow start, with only about 1,500 students taking advantage of the vouchers.[4] A fraction (about 25%) of Cleveland's vouchers were offered to families with children already in private schools, and vouchers in Cleveland could be used in religious schools, as they later could in the expanded Milwaukee program. About 80% of families in the Cleveland program sent their children to Catholic and other parochial schools.

Nearly all of the others went to Hope Schools—two private for-profit schools created by David Brennan, a wealthy entrepreneur and major contributor to Ohio's Republican Party, to take advantage of voucher availability. Brennan had been instrumental in getting the voucher program through the Ohio legislature, but was later unable to raise the value of the voucher once he realized that his schools were losing money at the $2,500 level. He subsequently converted the Hope Schools into charters to take advantage of higher levels of financing. This left almost all voucher students attending religious schools. On December 11, 2000, the 6th Circuit Federal Court of Appeals upheld a lower court ruling that these vouchers gave unconstitutional aid to religious schools. The program's future will be decided by the U.S. Supreme Court.

Evaluations of Cleveland vouchers are in even greater disagreement than the Milwaukee analyses. In Cleveland, almost as soon as the voucher program got under way, evaluations were conducted on different sets of students by two different groups of researchers. The Ohio legislature contracted researchers from the University of Indiana, headed by Kim Metcalf, to conduct the state's evaluation. Metcalf et al. could get "baseline" spring 1996 second-grade state test scores for almost all public school pupils. So the researchers focused on the almost 200 third-grade pupils who had received a voucher and switched from public to private schools in fall of 1996 (Metcalf et. al. 1998). They used as their outcome measure the scores on a test they gave to entire third-grade classrooms that contained their sample students.

Independently, the Peterson group (Greene, Howell, and Peterson) was also evaluating the Cleveland voucher program, but it focused on the two Hope Schools and looked at students in all grades, not just the third. The Peterson group did not collect data on previous tests taken by voucher students, but rather estimated increases in scores by comparing scores on tests *they* gave students in fall 1996 with scores on the same test in spring 1997. Greene et al. found higher levels of parent satisfaction in the Hope Schools and significant test score gains from fall 1996 to spring 1997 by students who started in one of grades K-3 in 1996 (Greene, Howell, and Peterson 1998). These findings were almost immediately criticized for using as baseline a test given right after the summer, when students have "lost" skills learned in the previous year (AFT 1997).

Because the Peterson group had already given tests twice in the Hope Schools (fall and spring), the schools' administration declined to test the children again using the Metcalf group's instrument. Metcalf et al. had to do a separate analysis of the Hope students. Their results of the second-grade test scores suggest that those students who used vouchers to get into non-Hope and Hope schools were similar socioeconomically to the sample taken of students remaining in Cleveland public schools, but they had higher initial test scores than public school students (these differences were not large). Metcalf et al.'s results for the 94 non-Hope School third-grade voucher students for whom they had second-grade scores showed no significant differences in the gains posted by voucher students and students who stayed in public schools, once socioeconomic background differences were accounted for.

The Peterson group was able to obtain Metcalf's data and almost immediately criticized the researchers' results on three main grounds: they limited their analysis to third graders, they used a second-grade test taken in public school the previous year that is not an accurate measure of baseline test scores, and they left the Hope Schools out of the analysis. They also claimed that Metcalf et al. used a statistical technique that underestimated treatment effects. But when the Peterson group reanalyzed Metcalf's data not taking into account second-grade scores, it found significant gains only for private school students in language and science. Controlling for second-grade test scores, even these gains were statistically insignificant at the 5% significance level (Peterson, Greene, and Howell 1998).

Yet another study by the Peterson group confirms that reported gains for students in the Hope Schools depend heavily on the low scores on the initial test in fall 1996. Any later scores compared with those initial test scores result in substantial reported gains, but using spring 1997 as a base results in consistent declines in math and reading scores for students in the Hope Schools (Peterson, Howell, and Greene 1999).

The Metcalf group continued to evaluate the voucher plan, following the third-grade cohort into fourth grade and testing the large cohort of voucher students in first grade. As in Milwaukee, the attrition rate from private schools was substantial from the first to the second year of the program.[5] Second-year results showed that fourth-grade voucher students in the established, non-Hope private schools scored significantly higher than did public school students in language and science but not in other subjects. Students in the Hope Schools, however, scored significantly lower in all subjects than did either public school students or voucher students in non-Hope Schools (Metcalf et al. 1999). The differences in scores between voucher students in non-Hope Schools and public school students were lower when socioeconomic differences were taken into account, but Hope students still had significantly lower scores. As was the case in Milwaukee, Metcalf et al. found that private school classes were marked by fewer students per teacher than were classes in public schools.

To summarize, the Milwaukee and Cleveland research on the effect of vouchers showed anywhere from no effects to small effects of vouchers for mainly African American student groups. Studies in Cleveland suggest that the achievement gains after two years in existing (religious) schools for voucher students were higher in one subject (science). Voucher students in for-profit private schools (the Hope Schools) did significantly worse than non-voucher students in one study (Metcalf et al.), but did better and then worse according to another study (Greene et al.).

Significantly, in both cities, different researchers, taking somewhat different approaches to the data, came up with different results. And in both cities, the Peterson group's evaluation of the voucher program reported the largest gains for students in private schools.

The new voucher research

The Peterson group's new round of research concerns efforts by well-financed voucher advocates to fund scholarships (vouchers) for low-income children to attend private schools. The programs establish lotteries for parents who apply, give applicants a baseline test, award scholarships to applicants at random, then later test children who did and did not receive the scholarships. Some families who get vouchers do not actually send their children to private school, either because they cannot come up with the extra tuition or because they cannot find convenient private schools to accept their children.[6]

Results for Dayton, New York, and Washington show no significant test score gains for Hispanic and white voucher recipients. Gains in the Howell et al. study are reported as National Percentile Ranking (NPR) points, which run from 0 to 100, with a national median of 50. This measurement allows the gains to be compared with test score gains reported in other studies, such as the Tennessee class size experiment. Gains for African Americans are found to be statistically significant overall in New York and Washington and marginally significant in reading in Dayton.[7] Reported gains are largest in Washington, D.C. (**Table 1**). As shown in **Figure A**, the aggregate math gain for African Americans across the three cities is about 5.5 percentile points in year 1. But math scores fail to increase significantly in year 2. The reading gain is negligible in year 1 and is about 6 percentile points in year 2. As shown in Table 1, gains for other ethnic groups are not significantly different from zero in either years 1 or 2.

Gains can also be expressed relative to the statistical variance of test scores in the sample of African Americans taking the test. This is called the "effect size." Gains are expressed in the proportion of a standard deviation in test score represented by the percentile point gains. One standard deviation is the difference in score between the average score (50th percentile)

TABLE 1 Impact on test score performance in three cities of switching to a private school (gain measured in National Percentile Ranking points)

	African American pupils				All other ethnic groups			
	Year 1		Year 2		Year 1		Year 2	
City/ grade/test	Gain	Sample size	Gain	Sample size	Gain	Sample size	Gain	Sample size
New York								
Grade 2/5								
Math	7.0***	623	4.1*	497	-2.1	817	-3.2	497
Reading	4.6**	623	4.5**	497	-1.3	817	0.2	497
D.C.								
Overall								
Math	7.3**	891	9.9***	700	8.5	39	5.8	44
Reading	-9.0**	891	8.1**	700	6.3	39	-5.6	44
Grade 2/5								
Math	9.8***	620	10.0***	490				
Reading	-5.1	620	8.6**	490				
Grade 6/8								
Math	1.5	270	12.8*	210				
Reading	-19.0***	270	7.8	210				
Dayton								
Grade 2/8								
Math	0.4	296	5.3	273	-0.8	108	0.0	96
Reading	6.1	296	7.6*	273	2.8	108	-0.4	96

* statistically significant at 10% level
** significant at 5% level
*** significant at 1% level
Note: Grade signifies grade entered in first year of study.

Source: Howell, Wolf, Peterson, and Campbell (2000), Tables 2A, 2B, and 2C.

and the 84th percentile on the up side or the 16th percentile on the down side. If the gain represents one-fourth of a standard deviation, it means, approximately, a move from the 50th to the 60th percentile. The percentile point gains for African Americans in Figure A translate into 0.3 standard deviations for math in year 1, with little if no gain in year 2, and, for reading, little gain in year 1 but about a 0.25 standard deviation effect size in year 2.

As shown in **Figure B**, if the major increase in math gains by D.C. middle school students between years 1 and 2 (from negligible to high positive gains) is excluded from the aggregate, the math gains for blacks decline between year 1 and year 2. Furthermore, if the huge turnaround in reading scores among D.C. elementary and middle school students is excluded from the aggregate, Dayton plus New York reading scores show a negligible aggregate gain after year 1.[8]

FIGURE A Test score gains for African Americans switching to a private school, New York, Washington, and Dayton

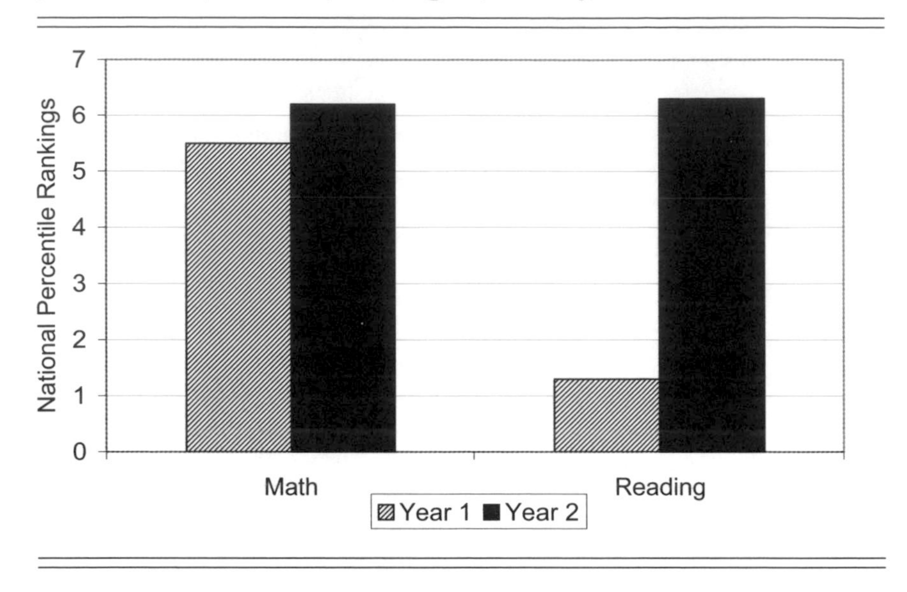

FIGURE B Test score gains for African Americans switching to a private school, Washington gains omitted

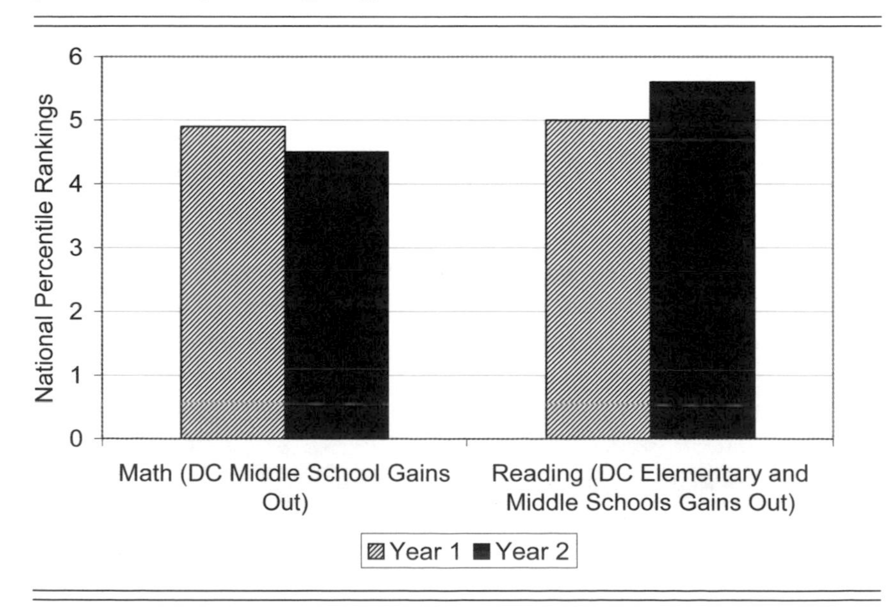

Source for figures A and B: see note to Table 1.

Thus, the combined results from two cities, Dayton and New York, suggest that for African American students the main effect of switching to a private school occurs in the year after the switch, and, as shown in Table 1, for other ethnic group (mainly Hispanic) students there is no effect at all. Using the same methodology, the Charlotte gains (not shown in table) are found to be about 6 percentile points in both reading and math. These are not broken down by ethnic group, but 80% of the sample is African American (Greene 2000).

Closer scrutiny

Several methodological issues make these comparisons of achievement gains problematic.

The 'disappointment' and Hawthorne effects problem. Comparing students already in public and private schools has a major disadvantage: private school students may come from more motivated families and have survived selection processes. Solving this problem requires an "experiment:" randomly assigning students to private and public schools.

The Peterson group draws on the statewide Tennessee class size experiment (Mosteller 1995) for much of the experimental method it uses to test the effects of vouchers. In Tennessee, students and teachers were randomly assigned to "normal" size classes (about 24 students) or classes reduced to about 15 students. All the students were followed and tested over the next 12 years. Researchers were able to distinguish those students who had stayed for several years in small classes, the students who had spent only one year in a small class and then switched, and the control group—those who stayed in normal size classes from kindergarten through the third grade. The Tennessee experiment, while randomly choosing the "treatment" (small class) and "control" groups (usual number of pupils in the classroom), was not a "blind" trial, as many medical experiments are. In a truly blind trial controls are given a placebo and do not know whether they are receiving the treatment. Education experiments can never fulfill this condition—families know their child's class size or whether they get a voucher. This makes education experiments subject to a "Hawthorne effect," where the fact that participants know they are involved in a treatment to produce a positive impact can cause them to try harder. The motivation of families who were rejected for the treatment (i.e., the controls) can also be affected by the experiment itself.

The voucher experiments in various cities have families apply for a voucher, give baseline tests to all applicants, then randomly select some to get vouchers to attend private schools.[9] But the students in these experiments are not necessarily representative of low-income urban students. Families applying for vouchers whose children attend public schools are more motivated to switch their children and more dissatisfied with public schools than are average low-income parents, most of whom do not apply. Not receiving a voucher for parents already dissatisfied with their child's schooling could have an adverse "disappointment" effect on the child's performance. [10]

The differential gains recorded in these experiments may therefore be due partly to lower gains by discouraged voucher rejectees rather than greater gains by recipients. Stanford psychologist Claude Steele has done research showing that test scores are significantly affected by the self-perception of test-takers (Steele and Aronson 1998). Although pupils who did not get a voucher were selected randomly, they and their parents may still feel "unlucky" and less efficacious. For a better comparison, voucher experiments would need also to draw a random sample of pupils from urban public schools whose low-income parents do not apply for vouchers, and give them the initial and follow-up tests. These pupils would come from families who are probably more satisfied with their current situation.

Peterson and Howell (2001) have responded to this criticism by claiming that the level of satisfaction with their children's public schooling by those parents who did not receive a voucher did not decline significantly in the first year following the voucher lottery, but it did in the second. Neither did rejected parents' participation rate in school activities decline. Since the chance of getting a voucher was only one in 20, it is not likely, the authors argue, that getting rejected produces any "sore loser" effect. But this is not very convincing. Peterson and Howell fail to mention that parents who applied for the voucher had rather low satisfaction with their children's schooling to start with. Continued low levels of satisfaction (or even declines after two years) may be enough to affect their children's test scores negatively.

Peterson and Howell also claim that, although there are some signs of a Hawthorne effect, the gains continue to increase in year 2 for African Americans, a trend which suggests that voucher gains persist and are not the result of a Hawthorne effect. The claim that the test score gains persist are based mainly on a large D.C. turnaround in second-year middle school math scores and second-year elementary and middle school reading scores. When these are excluded, there is no second-year increase (see Figure B).

Non-returnees at follow-up. Another problem is self-selection for the follow-up evaluation. Voucher researchers measure academic gains by convincing families to bring children in on a weekend to take follow-up math and reading tests. As in medical trials, high participation rates may require inducements. For those families who received vouchers, the New York inducement was that children would have to take the test to continue getting a voucher. Researchers used only moral suasion in other cities. For those who received but did not use the voucher and for those in the control group (who did not get a voucher), the inducement was typically $20 plus eligibility for a voucher in the future. Participation rates varied, with the highest rates in New York (about 66% in the second-year follow-up) and about 50% in D.C. and Dayton. The participation rate in Charlotte was particularly low, at 40%. All these are considerably lower than in medical trials.

The Peterson group deals with participation problems by estimating the probability that a student with a certain initial test score and set of family characteristics and attitudes would participate in each follow-up test and then weighting actual scores according to this probability. Probability functions were estimated separately for the control group and for those who received vouchers, using data researchers had gathered on the original questionnaires and the original test scores for all the students who had applied to be in the program. Using these probability functions, the students actually participating in the follow-up tests received a weight that was the inverse of the probability that a student with those characteristics would come back and take a follow-up test. For example, if a student had a set of parent characteristics that made it likely that he/she would participate in the follow-up, he/she was given a lower weight in the calculation of the estimated follow-up test. Thus, students who came back to take follow-up tests but had characteristics that made them unlikely follow-up participants got a bigger weight, so test scores would be more "representative" of the original group of students.

The researchers could not do much more than this to correct for no-shows. But the procedure is hardly free of potential bias. It assumes that follow-up test scores for the many who didn't take the tests would be the same as scores for those who did show up and had similar initial scores and similar parent characteristics. But we really don't know how follow-up scores of no-shows might be related to their not showing up to take the follow-up test. For example, those who did not show up to take the first-year or second-year follow-ups may have had indications from their performance during the school year that they might score low, even though they did reasonably well on the baseline test. This might have been especially true for private school students, or, alternatively, for public school students. Thus, the large non-participation rates could easily have reflected behavior that systematically biased the relative gains of voucher recipients and non-recipients.

Bias issues in taking up the voucher offer. Yet another problem is bias in who takes up the voucher offer. The vouchers, which range from $1,200 to $1,700, depending on the city, are not large enough to cover tuition at most of the private schools available. Many families receiving vouchers were unable to use them. In New York, 62% of families whose children started out in public school used the scholarships for two years; in Dayton and Washington, 53% used the voucher in the first year, with an unreported drop-off in the second year.

Voucher takers in each city, as would be expected, have higher income than non-takers. Critics have argued that this income difference biases results. But the researchers have made a valid attempt to deal with the problem by comparing the controls with all students who were offered the voucher, not only those who actually used it. Here is how it works. Those who receive a voucher and use it may be self-selecting when they choose to go to private school—they may be the better students from higher-educated families, with greater chances to make test score gains. But voucher recipients are randomly chosen, so a good "instrument" in this case is whether the student received a voucher—if there is a major difference between voucher recipients and users, the "instrument" should pick that up. To test whether the measured or unmeasured characteristics of voucher users would produce such a result, the researchers estimated the private school effect conditioned on the probability that someone who got a voucher actually used it.[11]

The single cohort problem. In New York, the only students who made significant gains were African Americans who switched to private schools when they were entering the fifth grade and whose gains were large enough to produce a significant average gain for the entire New York sample of African Americans.

Results for African American students in Dayton also have a strange inconsistency. Certain cohorts—those who entered second, fourth, and sixth grades in the first year of the experiment—had large National Percentile Ranking percentage-point gains in combined math and reading test scores for the two years in private schools, while those in the other grades did not. According to David Howell (who kindly provided unpublished data by grade), African American voucher recipients finishing private school third grades at the end of the study's second year made large two-year gains (in combined math and reading). Those finishing fourth grade performed slightly worse than pupils who did not get vouchers. Those finishing private school fifth grades made large gains, those finishing private school sixth grades made small losses, those finishing seventh grade made large gains, and

TABLE 2 Two-year test score gains for African American students from switching to private schools in Dayton and Washington, math and reading combined, by grade (National Percentile Ranking points)

Grade (in second year of trial)	Dayton point estimate	D.C. point estimate
3	19.7	10.2
4	-1.9	8.1
5	14.5	3.5
6	-1.8	9.7
7	17.0	11.4
8	-5.7	4.0
9	-14.9	-3.6

Source: Data provided to author by William G. Howell.

those finishing eighth and ninth grades made large losses compared to non-voucher students. Only in Washington, D.C. are achievement gains of voucher recipients attending private schools relatively consistent across grades (**Table 2**).With gains so variable by cohort, it is fair to ask, as did Mathematica's David Myers *(New York Times,* September 2000) concerning his New York study for the Peterson group, whether one can claim that students in private schools do better than those in public schools. Shouldn't we, instead, wonder what conditions produced such large gains for some cohorts but not for others?

Tankers and leapers. First-year results were reported in 1999. In Dayton and Washington, D.C., the first-year estimates in those earlier reports excluded "tankers" (test takers whose scores fell more than 1.5 standard deviations) and "leapers" (test takers whose scores rose more than 2 standard deviations). In the more recent second-year report, tankers and leapers are not excluded, changing the first-year results considerably. For example, the 7% gain in math scores reported in year 1 for black students in Dayton is reduced to zero. The Washington math score gain in grades 2-5 rises from 7% in the first-year report to 10% in the latest report, and the reading score in grades 6-8 drops from –8% to –19%. The rationale for not excluding leapers and tankers from the second round of estimates is that, if they stayed high or low, it indicated a more "permanent" effect. But the sample size in both Dayton and Washington dropped considerably in the second year, particularly among African Americans in Washington and highest of all in the highly volatile Washington grades 6-8. How was this drop in sample size related to tankers and leapers? Did more "divers" among voucher students not show up for the second round of testing? Did more tankers and other low-scoring students leave private schools at the end of the first year, as occurred in Cleveland (Metcalf et al. 1999)? If so, this could have affected the results as to gains in scores. One simple way to test for this would be to present second-year results with tankers and leapers excluded, giving readers an insight into the robustness of the results.

Erratic results. A final problem is erratic results. Big differences between first- and second-year gains in Washington, D.C. may relate to which students failed to show up for testing in the second year. Students might have failed to participate in the second-year testing either because of negative first-year experiences in private schools, or because of disappointment with the first-year testing result. For such students, the probability is higher that they would do badly again than that they would do well. If they leave the sample, that alone could drive up the second-year result.

Chapter 2

Do vouchers improve failing public schools?

In the latest round of voucher advocacy research, Jay Greene, another member of the Peterson group, recently announced that the threat of vouchers in Florida for students in "failing" public schools caused math and writing gains among Florida's lowest-performing schools to increase significantly more than the gains of higher-performing schools (Greene 2001a). The finding was widely publicized as "proving" that vouchers were an effective policy tool for improving education.

In 1999, Florida adopted the A+ accountability system, which included a provision that awarded vouchers to students in schools that "failed" repeatedly. Florida grades schools as A, B, C, D, or F, based on the average scores students achieve on the Florida Comprehensive Assessment Test (FCAT). If a school receives Fs two out of four years, it becomes eligible for some form of corrective action, including but not limited to the offer of vouchers to its students to attend other schools, public or private. In the 1999-2000 school year, two Pensacola schools met the failing criteria and lost 53 children to private schools and 85 children to other public schools.

Greene used results on reading, math, and writing tests by school for the years 1998-99 and 1999-2000 to test the notion that "performance of students on academic tests improves when public schools are faced with the prospect that their students will receive vouchers" (Greene 2001a, 2). He finds that all 78 schools that received an F grade in 1999 (66 primary schools, seven middle schools, and four high schools) received a higher grade in 2000. The gains by F schools were also much higher than those for schools ranked A-D. To get the "voucher effect," Greene compares schools that "were probably very much alike in many respects" (Greene 2001a, 7), namely higher-scoring F schools and lower-scoring D schools. [12] The only thing that differentiates these two types of schools, according to Greene, is that the F's have the threat of vouchers hanging over them, and the D's do not. He concludes from this comparison that the higher-scoring F schools did significantly better on the math and writing tests, with "effect sizes" (the difference in high F and low D scores compared to the standard deviation of the scores in the sample of schools being compared) of 0.12 for reading, 0.30 for math, and 0.41 for writing. This difference, he claims, is the effect that can be assigned to the voucher threat.

Part of this difference, Greene recognizes, may be due to an effect known as "regression to the mean." We would expect that individuals or groups of individuals scoring particularly low in one year would score higher in the next year, not because of any action taken but because of simple variation in performance. Similarly, high scorers in any year are likely to score lower in the following year. Baseball batting averages are a good example of this phenomenon. Players who have been in the majors for several years and had bad years in 1999 will, on average, have higher batting averages in 2000, not necessarily because of the threat of being sent to the minors (even though that threat exists), but because the normal variation associated with batting over a whole season makes it likely that hitters doing badly in a given year will do better rather than worse. The opposite is true for players who had particularly good years. Greene checks for this phenomenon by comparing gains of higher-scoring F schools with lower-scoring F schools. He finds that in reading and math, the higher-scoring F schools have higher gains than lower-scoring F schools. On these grounds, he dismisses the regression to the mean effect.

The Greene analysis has major defects that fall into two categories. First, his statistical analysis tends to overestimate the effect of being designated an F school. His interpretation of the size effects is also probably too large. Second, whatever the correct test score gain caused by a school getting an F grade, Greene presents no evidence that this should be attributed to the threat of vouchers. Florida's school-grading program is relatively new, but was in effect before 1999, the year the voucher threat was first used. How much larger was the effect in that year compared to previous years, when an F designation carried stigma but no voucher threat? Greene does not answer this question, but the data are available to do so. Other states, such as Texas and North Carolina, also have "scarlet letter" designations that trigger sanctions but not vouchers. Do F-graded schools in those states make larger gains than D schools?

Mis-estimating the 'scarlet letter' effect. Gregory Camilli and Katrina Bulkley (2001), professors at Rutgers University, re-estimated the differential gains of F-designated schools, using the same database available to Greene. They chose to compare *all* students who took the test rather than just the "standard" student population (which excludes "special" categories of students) used by Greene. There is no reason to believe that this changes the estimated gains, although Greene argues that F schools are likely to have more special students when all students are included, dampening their estimated gains compared to gains when only standard students are included. However, a deeper problem exists: FCAT may have been given to two different populations of students in 1998-99 and 1999-2000.[13] In the earlier year, *all* students in school at the time of the test (in early spring) were given the test. In 1999-2000, only those students who were enrolled in that particular school in October took the FCAT. This would tend to increase test score gains because students who have been in school all year are likely to do better on the test than are students who changed schools during the year. This is particularly true for low-income students who are more likely to attend low-scoring schools (Rumberger 1996). This selection bias alone would cast doubt on Greene's results.

Yet, Camilli and Bulkley raise three other objections to Greene's statistical treatment of the data. They argue that Greene inadequately corrects for regression to the mean; that he aggregates data across primary, middle, and high schools; and that he overestimates size effects by inappropriately using the standard deviation of school mean test scores as the reference variable instead of the much larger variation of student test scores. In Greene's answer to Camilli and Bulkley, he rejects all three criticisms. Who is right?

Greene interprets the regression-to-the-mean problem as a floor effect (when scores are very low, they can only go up). However, as Camilli and Bulkley correctly point out, regression to the mean is not mainly the result of a floor effect but of "noise"—unexplainable variation that tends to raise low scores and reduce high scores in any give year toward the mean the next year. Camilli and Bulkley correct for this effect by (1) estimating the predicted school test score in year 2 as a function of school test score in year 1, (2) calculating the gain between second-year score and predicted second-year score, and (3) estimating the relation between this gain and school designations (in A, B, C, D, and F categories). They argue that this gives a "truer" estimate of the effect of school designation, corrected for gains associated with regression to the mean. Greene claims that their form of estimation "overcorrects" for the potential voucher effect because it "takes away" part of the gain of F-designated schools that could have come as a response to vouchers. He would be right if there were little noise in school test scores in a given year, so that all or almost all of the variation were due to policy effects such as school designation. But given what we know about school test score variation from year to year, this is unlikely.

Since Greene sees the regression-to-the-mean problem as a floor effect, he tries to test for it by comparing the gains of low-scoring F-designated schools with high-scoring F-designated schools. He finds no significant differences in reading and math score gains between those schools, but significantly larger gains in writing for low-scoring F schools. He concludes that there is no regression-to-the-mean effect and that the F designation itself (the voucher threat) is the main explanation for the larger gain of low-scoring schools. But Haggai Kupermintz, a statistician at the University of Colorado, shows that low-scoring schools within all groups (A, B, C, D, E, and F) make larger gains than high-scoring schools in reading and math, and, that in math and especially writing, low-scoring F schools make much larger gains than high-scoring F schools (Kupermintz 2001, Fig. 2). Yet, even correcting for regression to the mean, Camilli and Bulkley and Kupermintz find a significant effect on math and writing achievement gain associated with the F designation. The estimated effect is not much different from the one Greene estimates when he compares the gains of high-scoring F-designated schools and low-scoring D-designated schools—what he calls the "hard" voucher effect.

The question of whether or not it is proper to divide the analysis into levels of schooling depends on what one wants to know. Camilli and Bulkley's analysis tells us that the big gains in both reading and math are in the seven middle schools that received an F designation. Middle schools made smaller relative gains in writing. High schools that received F's actually went down relative to other schools in math and reading and made about the same gains in writing, and primary schools with F designations made large relative gains in writing, smaller relative gains in math, and no relative gains in reading. Thus, the underlying results by school level and academic area suggest that an F designation has, at best, an uneven impact across school levels and subject areas. Greene's analysis aggregates these results, gaining some statistical significance but losing interesting and important information.

Should the size effects be measured in terms of the variance of scores among schools or among individual students? This depends on the kinds of comparisons being made. If we want to compare effect sizes of gains on different tests within the sample of Florida schools, Greene's use of test score variance among schools is a valid reference for effect size. But that is not the comparison Greene makes. He argues that educational researchers consider "effect sizes of 0.1 to 0.2 standard deviations to be small, effects of 0.3 to 0.4 standard deviations as moderate, and gains of 0.5 or more standard deviations are thought of as large" (Greene 2001a, 8). These are effect sizes based on gains compared to the variation of *individual* student achievement scores, which are much larger than the variation of average school scores. If the gains associated with receiving an F designation are to be compared with, for example, the effect size of the Tennessee class size reduction experiment (as Greene does), he is claiming an effect on *students* in F schools of a net six-point gain in math scores (Camilli and Bulkley estimate a smaller gain). This gain, to be comparable to the effect sizes of educational research on individual student gains, should be compared to the standard deviation of individual student scores in the FCAT, not of school scores. This makes the effect size of the math gains in F-designated schools quite small (less than 0.1 standard deviations) and the writing gains moderate (about 0.23), as noted in the Camilli and Bulkley critique.

Incorrectly attributing gains at F schools to the threat of vouchers. Throughout Greene's analysis, he claims that the higher gains of F schools (corrected for regression to the mean) must be the result of voucher threat. However, F schools may also tend to raise their test scores more than other schools in other situations where there is no voucher threat. Being branded an F school may itself carry sufficient stigma to cause F schools to raise their test scores, whether or not there is a voucher threat. If that is the case, we (and Greene) have no way of knowing whether vouchers were the cause of higher scores in Florida in 1999-2000.

One way to test that hypothesis is to estimate the net effect of the F designation in Florida in the years before the voucher threat. Another is to make similar estimates for other states that rate schools as failing. Although Greene did not correct properly in his analysis for regression to the mean, it is worth comparing the relative performance of F schools to non-failing schools in these other situations using Greene's flawed methodology. This simulates what Greene might have found were he to do his (flawed) statistical analysis in Florida before the A+ plan was implemented, or in Texas or North Carolina, which have no statewide voucher program.

Data are available on school performance in Florida beginning in 1996-97, a year after the state implemented a testing program and categorized schools by the proportion of students passing the state tests. Doug Harris has analyzed these data and compared them to Greene's results for the first year of the A+ program (see Appendix A for the complete Harris study). Harris also compares his and Greene's results using Camilli and Bulkley's corrections for potential regression to the mean.

Table 3 presents Greene's and Harris' results using the regression to the mean using Greene's method of comparing the gains of high-scoring F schools to the gains of low-scoring D schools. Harris uses 1997-98 gains (pre-voucher), and Greene uses 1999-2000 gains (post-voucher). The gains in math at F schools before vouchers were introduced were larger than in the post-voucher years, but gains in reading and writing are larger post-voucher. In **Table 4** Harris adjusts both his and Greene's estimates for re-

TABLE 3 Adjusting for regression to the mean, Greene's approach (effect size)

	Harris: Florida ratings (1997-98)			Greene: Florida A+ (1999-2000)		
	Reading	Math	Writing	Reading	Math	Writing
Low 2 (D)	0.097	0.142	0.817	0.184	0.259	0.694
High 1 (F)	0.053	0.374	0.856	0.222	0.346	0.882
Difference	-0.044	+0.132	+0.039	+0.038	+0.087	+0.186

Source: Harris, Appendix A.

TABLE 4 Adjusting for regression to the mean, Camilli and Bulkley approach

	Harris: Florida grading			Greene: Florida A+		
	Reading	Math	Writing	Reading	Math	Writing
4 (A+B)	+0.012	+0.023	+0.041	+0.029	+0.005	NA
3 (C)	- 0.009	- 0.026	- 0.041	-0.001	- 0.000	NA
2 (D)	- 0.031	- 0.082	- 0.151	-0.001	- 0.025	NA
1 (F)	- 0.040	+0.199	- 0.091	+0.021	+0.062	NA

Source: Harris, Appendix A.

TABLE 5 Isolating the effect of a low-performance rating, Texas

	Gains in reading	Number	Gains in math	Number
Lower-scoring 'acceptable'	1.4212	1,338	2.1548	560
Higher-scoring 'low performing'	1.5417	45	3.8719	62
Low-performance effect	0.1205		1.1717	
Low-performance effect measured in standard deviations	0.018		0.184	
Low-performance effect in Florida measured in standard deviations	0.12		0.30	

Note: Gains are measured in terms of the Texas Learning Index, set at 70 for the minimum-expected learning level in each grade.

Source: Brownson; see Appendix B.

gression to the mean using the Camilli and Bulkley approach. Again, the math gains were much larger for F schools before the voucher threat, and reading gains were slightly larger relative to other schools once vouchers were introduced. If vouchers were the reason that F-designated schools did so much better in 1999-2000, as Greene claims, it is difficult to understand why F schools made larger (and significant) relative gains in math without any voucher sanction and why reading skills made insignificant gains even with a voucher sanction.

Amanda Brownson of the University of Texas' Dana Center duplicated the Greene analysis for Texas schools (see Appendix B). She compared the gains on the Texas Assessment of Academic Skills (TAAS) between the academic years 1996-97 and 1997-98 and the years 1998-99 and 1999-2000 for "low-performing" designated schools (this corresponds to the F designation in Florida) with "exemplary," "recognized," and "acceptable" schools' gains. Brownson argues that, because the Texas assessment is older than Florida's, schools in Texas have been making gains over a longer period than in Florida. She shows that TAAS scores increased steadily throughout the 1990s, but tailed off by 1999-2000. For both sets of comparisons of gains in scores, she found similar results for Texas as Greene found in Florida, even though Texas has no voucher threat.[14]

When Brownson compares the gains in lower-scoring "acceptable" schools with higher-scoring low-performance schools in 1998-99/1999-2000, she finds a very small net effect for low-performing schools in reading gains but a larger, statistically significant effect in math score gains. In both tests, the effect sizes are smaller than in Florida (here it is appropriate to compare relative gains to the standard deviation in mean scores among schools in order to correspond to the Greene results). These results are shown in **Table 5**. (Note that Brownson divides the test score gains by the standard deviation based on Greene's approach. Therefore, Tables 5 and 6 below should not be compared with Tables 3 and 4 above.)

Table 6 shows the same comparison for the early years. The difference in higher-scoring low-performance schools and lower-performing acceptable schools is statistically significant for both reading and math scores, and the effect sizes are close to the effect sizes estimated by Greene for Florida. Brownson's argument that gains were likely to be larger for low-performing schools in earlier years is borne out. More important, her estimates show that, using Greene's methodology, the level of relative gains made by failing schools in Florida is also made by failing schools in Texas, *although Texas uses no voucher threat.* Brownson also corrected her estimates for regression to the mean, using the Camilli-Bulkley method. This correction strengthens her conclusion that failing schools in Texas made

TABLE 6 Isolating the effect of a low-performance rating, 1996-97

	Gains in reading	Number	Gains in math	Number
Lower-scoring 'acceptable'	2.5565	1,714	3.3672	1,750
Higher-scoring 'low performing'	3.1990	55	4.6690	55
Low-performance effect	0.6425		1.3018	
The Texas low-performance effect measured in standard deviations	0.115		0.243	
The Florida voucher effect measured in standard deviations	0.12		0.30	

Note: Gains are measured in terms of the Texas Learning Index, set at 70 for the minimum-expected learning level in each grade.

Source: Brownson; see Appendix B.

relative gains as large or larger than the gains Greene attributes to Florida's voucher plan.[15] Like Florida and Texas, North Carolina has a "strong" accountability system that sanctions schools for continued "low performance." In North Carolina, the four main categories of schools are "exemplary," "meets expectations," "no recognition," and "low performing." Sanctions in North Carolina also do *not* include the threat of vouchers. Duke University's Helen Ladd, a well-known public policy analyst who has written about accountability (Ladd 1996) and about choice in New Zealand (Fiske and Ladd 2000), duplicated Greene's analysis for North Carolina (see Appendix C). She grouped schools into the four categories used by the state to characterize school performance over time[16] and examined two different measures of changes in student performance by school from 1997 to 1998: the change in the percent of students at or above grade level in each year of school based on reading, math, and writing scores (performance composite), and the gain in test scores minus the expected gain in test scores in each year (growth composite). These are the two standards by which schools in North Carolina are judged.

Ladd found that, for both measures of change, "low-performing" schools had a significantly greater positive change than any other school type (**Tables 7A** and **7B**). She also duplicated Greene's Florida comparison of high-scoring "low-performing" schools with low-scoring "no-recognition" schools. This comparison in North Carolina shows that high-scoring low-performing schools had a higher gain on both measures of gain than did no-recognition schools, and this difference was statistically significant (**Tables 8A** and **8B**). Ladd concludes that in North Carolina low-perform-

TABLE 7A Changes in performance composite, North Carolina, 1997-98

1997 school evaluation	Avg. difference in composite	Number of schools
Exemplary	2.37	514
Expected growth	3.43	380
No recognition	4.94	551
Low performing	10.68	114

TABLE 7B Changes in growth composite, North Carolina, 1997-98

1997 school evaluation	Avg. difference in composite	Number of schools
Exemplary	2.11	514
Expected growth	4.66	380
No recognition	7.48	551
Low performing	10.98	114

The change for low-performing schools compared to schools with higher evaluations is statistically significant at $p<.0001$.

Source: Ladd and Glennie, Appendix C.

TABLE 8A Changes in performance composite, North Carolina, 1997-98, comparing 'most similar' schools

1997 school evaluation	Avg. difference in composite	Number of schools
Lower-scoring no recognition	5.91	272
Higher-scoring low performing	9.22	57

TABLE 8B Changes in growth composite, North Carolina, 1997-98, comparing 'most similar' schools

1997 school evaluation	Avg. difference in composite	Number of schools
Lower-scoring no recognition	7.24	272
Higher-scoring low performing	9.46	57

The difference between the gains for the two school types is statistically significant at $p<.0001$.

Source: Ladd and Glennie, Appendix C.

ing schools made significantly larger achievement gains than other school categories, *with no voucher threat.*

Thus, Greene's claim that vouchers caused the observed gains in Florida may or may not be true, but the evidence he presents is not sufficient to support his case. We observe that schools designated as failing in Florida before the A+ voucher plan was implemented showed even larger gains in math scores. We also observe similarly large test score gains for schools designated as failing in states without vouchers. This suggests that using larger gains to Florida's F schools in 1999-2000 as evidence that a voucher threat improves low-performing public schools is at best a stretch.

In sum, Greene's statistical estimates have problems, but, more important, he should have been much more careful in attributing the larger gains he found for schools designated as failing to the voucher threat component of the Florida A+ plan. In studies that duplicate Greene's study for Florida in years before the A+ voucher plan was implemented, and in studies of Texas and North Carolina—states that publicize school "failure" but do not use a voucher threat—F-designated schools consistently make larger gains. Given these results, we have no reason to believe that the larger rise in student performance in low-performing schools in Florida in 1999-2000 was due to the threat of vouchers.

Parenthetically, we also cannot argue that the larger test score gains in failing schools in Texas and North Carolina were the result of those states' accountability systems. To prove any of these cases, we would have to show that individual schools' test scores behaved in a particular way over time and then changed significantly when the voucher threat or (in states without vouchers) other policies designed to change their behavior appeared.

Chapter 3

What have we learned?

Voucher evaluations in the U.S. have now gone through several phases. They all analyze voucher experiments aimed at low-income children, mostly African Americans, in medium and large cities, and now, with the Florida study, in states. The first experiments were publicly financed and offered vouchers by lottery. But vouchers were generally *under*-subscribed, and those applicants who did not receive vouchers were not necessarily randomly rejected nor carefully followed up. Thus, evaluations in the first phase generally chose as a "control" group students in public schools who resembled voucher students socioeconomically. These first-phase evaluations were also carried out using similar data by various researchers, some voucher advocates and others not.

The second plans were privately financed, and evaluations were designed to conform to medical experiments, where treatment and control groups are selected randomly. Vouchers were offered to a large group of low-income applicants by lottery. Vouchers were fully subscribed, and both voucher recipients and non-recipients were followed up with tests at the end of the first and second years of the experiment. In comparing pupils who receive vouchers to those who do not in this fashion, bias from differential motivation and socioeconomic background is allegedly eliminated.

The third round of studies have moved into the analysis of the effects of a voucher *threat* on low-performing public schools.

The results of the first round of studies in Milwaukee and Cleveland suggest that parents who receive vouchers and use them (actually send their children to private schools) are more satisfied with their schools than are parents of similar socioeconomic background whose children attend public schools. There is general agreement on that point. There is also general agreement that the vouchers enabled low-income parents who otherwise would not have been able to do so to send their children to private schools. Yet, the sample of low-income, urban parents seeking vouchers does not represent the average low-income urban parent with children in public school. Parents who file for vouchers are, for one, more dissatisfied than other parents. To determine whether private schools are more satisfying to low-income parents than public schools would require taking a random sample of all low-income parents in a particular city with children in public *and* private schools and randomly re-assigning students to public and private schools. Parents whose children were assigned to private schools might still be more satisfied than before, but the differences would probably be much smaller than when only the children of dissatisfied parents are switched.

The results are less clear on the achievement effects of vouchers in Milwaukee and Cleveland. Results varied according to which researchers did the studies. The Peterson group produced the most favorable results for vouchers in each of the two cities. When all the results are compared, it appears that voucher-using (choice) students in Milwaukee probably made greater gains by their third and fourth years in private schools—at least in math—than did students in public schools. But the achievement effect was not large, and only a fraction of voucher students stayed in private schools for this long even though the voucher fully covered tuition. In Cleveland, the most reliable results suggest that, after two years, choice students who used their vouchers to attend existing (religious) private schools made greater gains in science than did non-choice students but not in other subjects. Students who used their vouchers in the commercial schools created to take advantage of the voucher plan did significantly worse compared to other students, both students in public schools and voucher users in religious private schools. As in Milwaukee, attrition rates of voucher users from private schools were large over the first and second years of the program.

The Milwaukee and Cleveland cases also indicate that small vouchers of $2,500 or less, such as in the early years of the Milwaukee experiment and in Cleveland, limit the number of low-income families that will actually use the voucher, either because the families cannot supply the extra tuition or because the number of private schools made available at that level of voucher funding is too limited. The eventually much larger Milwaukee voucher increased the number of private schools entering the market and also apparently made the voucher more attractive to low-income families. Nevertheless, we have no information on how the greater number of Milwaukee voucher students are performing compared to their counterparts in Milwaukee's public schools.

The results from the second round of voucher studies show similar satisfaction gains as in Milwaukee and Cleveland, but much larger achievement gains from using a voucher in private schools, at least for African American students. Studies were available only to one set of researchers. All students attended existing private schools, many of them religious, which makes the favorable results not inconsistent with results in Cleveland, although they were still much larger in Dayton and particularly Washington, D.C.

The authors of the second round of studies claim that their results are better than those done in Milwaukee and Cleveland because of the truly experimental design of the evaluation. However, this strategy does not speak to other issues. The new studies suffer from uncorrected potential biases, including "disappointment effects" of families that did not receive vouchers, low participation rates in follow-up tests, the concentration of gains in particular small cohorts in the sample that the researchers do not attempt to explain, and possibly non-random declines in participation between baseline testing and the first and second years of follow-up testing.

The Peterson group cites Carolyn Hoxby's description of randomized field trials as the "gold standard" of social science research.[17] Hoxby's characterization certainly has merit. But to the extent that the Peterson group's results depend upon instrumental variables and upon weighting to correct for non-participation, they are no longer reporting results of a randomized field trial, but rather are reporting an empirical study with many of the dangers of assuming the relevance of characteristics that the "gold standard" attempts to avoid.

The Peterson group model has yet another problem. Low-income urban pupils attending private schools may do better because private schools are able to select their students. To the degree that a private school can construct a *peer* environment that is conducive to learning in ways that public schools cannot because they must take all comers, the influence of peers on student achievement may be more positive than in a public school. The ability to select students is not a feature of private education that voucher advocates care to stress, because, if this is the source of a positive private school effect, it can imply no condemnation of public schools that are unable to select students. Further, peer effects can run out quickly as private education expands in inner cities.[18] The Cleveland results showing small positive gains to voucher students who entered existing private religious schools and significant relative *declines* in test scores for students who used their vouchers in the commercial Hope Schools could be partly the result of peer effects, not just the relative quality of teaching in different types of schools.

The Peterson group could deal with this problem if it tested a random sample of students already in the private schools attended by voucher recipients, identified them by school, and estimated the peer effect (average test score of non-voucher students in each school) on the score of voucher recipients attending the school. It may not be easy to get the private schools to allow such testing, simply because they would then be subjecting themselves to evaluation. But without such information, it is difficult to understand the source of private school advantage, if such advantage even exists.

Peterson and his colleagues should have an interest in knowing whether it is peer effect or school characteristics that are producing their positive results for voucher students attending private schools. They claim, contrary to Cecilia Rouse's results in Milwaukee, that smaller class size is not an important factor in explaining the higher gains in private schools of African American students. Indeed, in a recent paper, they were unable to explain why, in New York City, African American students realized a positive effect on test scores from attending a private school while Latino students did not. Private school characteristics as reported by parents, including class size, did not explain test score differences.[19] If peer effects are important in explaining whether students using vouchers make significant gains over their public school counterparts, then we might infer that a voucher plan is likely to benefit relatively few low-income students, i.e., mainly those who can get into existing schools with already better-performing students. Correspondingly, it should be kept in mind that small vouchers of $1,700 (New York City and Washington, D.C.) or $1,500 (President Bush's plan) would be unlikely to induce the creation of many new private schools for low-income voucher students.

Objective evaluations of the currently much larger Milwaukee voucher plan would provide additional information on the extent of voucher benefits. Since relatively large numbers of low-income students have apparently shifted from public to private schools (and some back), and voucher students attend approximately 100 different schools, it would be possible to assess differences in effects by type of school and whether gains are due to student selection or school quality.

In the study of competition effects, the voucher studies, as exemplified by Greene's Florida analysis, attempt to measure the "macro" effect of vouchers on public school improvement. These studies are more indirect than the studies of individual effects in experiments, so they require even more care in estimating voucher effects and interpreting them. Just the opposite has occurred. Jay Greene's study draws attention to Florida's voucher program, but tends to overestimate the degree to which failing schools actually do better than other types of schools and tells us little about whether the threat of vouchers actually makes low-performing public schools do better. Indeed, as the studies of relative gains made in an earlier year in Florida and by failing schools in Texas and North Carolina show, even without a voucher threat failing schools made relative gains as large or larger than in Florida in 1999-2000, when vouchers were introduced. If "failing" schools consistently make larger test score gains than higher-scoring schools in such a wide variety of situations, the fact that they did so in Florida in 1999-2000, when Florida's A+ voucher plan went into effect, is not evidence that the voucher threat was responsible for the larger gains. Much more rigorous empirical tests are required to make that case.

APPENDIX A

What caused the effects of the Florida A+ program: ratings or vouchers?

by Doug Harris, Economic Policy Institute

Criticisms of Jay Greene's analysis of the Florida A+ program fall into two categories: problems in estimating the effect size, and problems in attributing the effect size to the A+ program. This appendix focuses on the second problem. How much of the gain identified by Greene was caused by vouchers and how much was caused by the embarrassment of being labeled an "F" school?

It is often difficult to determine the effects of any individual policy. Governments often change multiple policies at the same time, making it difficult to understand which change had what impact. This same problem arises in the case of the A+ program. The state of Florida assigned labels to schools (A-F) *and* funded vouchers for schools that fell in the F category. This means that A+ is really two programs, which could have been implemented separately. Vouchers could have been funded regardless of school ratings, and the ratings could have been made without vouchers.

In November 1995, the Florida Department of Education (FDOE) released ratings to the public for each school in the state based on test scores from 1993-94 and 1994-95. Level 1 was called "critically low" and included 158 schools. The rules included *non-voucher* sanctions for schools that remained on this list for three consecutive years. However, these sanctions would only occur after three years and only after a series of hearings with the state Board of Education and appeals by the school district. Even if the district were found to be negligent through this process, the state board was not required to take action. Regardless, no sanctions were ever imposed.

Despite the apparent weakness of the sanction threat, anecdotal evidence suggests the schools worked hard to improve their scores to avoid further public embarrassment.[20] Many schools subsequently increased their ratings through test score improvement, decreasing the number of "critically low" schools from 158 to 71 in 1995-96 and to 30 in 1996-97.

In 1999, the state added a provision that students in schools designated as "failing" for two consecutive years would be offered a voucher that could be used in any other school, private or public. This was called the A+ program. At the beginning of the 1999-2000 school year, students in two schools were offered vouchers. They were chosen based on 1998 ratings and a "long history of failure," even though the two-consecutive-year provision of the A+ program was not yet in effect. In 2000-01, no schools qualified for vouchers; all the 1999-2000 F schools managed to rise to an acceptable rating.

The analysis here attempts to compare the effects of the pre-voucher ratings with the A+ program, which includes both ratings and vouchers. If the effects of the earlier ratings were similar to the ratings-plus-vouchers included in A+, then this would provide evidence that vouchers did not add much value.

Analysis

The general method used here is simple. First, the test score gains achieved by "critically low" schools due to the ratings released in 1995 are estimated. Second, these gains are compared to those of the F schools studied by Greene and others, which also had the threat of vouchers. The methodology follows closely the analysis by Greene (2001), Camilli and Bulkley (2001), Brownson (Appendix B), and Ladd and Glennie (Appendix C).

While the general method is simple, the implementation is somewhat more complicated. One potential problem is that different schools used different tests in both reading and math during 1995-97, just before the FCAT was introduced. In these subject areas, schools were allowed to select from a menu of nationally norm-referenced tests. This is a common circumstance in education research, and it is common practice to make the results comparable by using either percentiles or effect sizes (gains adjusted based on the standard deviation). In this case, the FDOE reports the percentage of students in the school who reach the national 50th percentile on whichever test was taken. The writing scores, in contrast to reading and math, are based on a single statewide test taken by all students. In this case, the FDOE reports the percentage of students who receive a "3" or higher. Therefore, in the case of writing, adjustments are not necessary to compare scores across schools.

One possible effect of the new tests is that schools may achieve gains by "teaching to the test," i.e., teaching test-taking techniques and focusing their teaching on the kinds of material covered in the state exams. This is much more likely after 1999, since major changes were made in Florida testing at about that time. Specifically, Florida created its own test, FCAT, which replaced the nationally normed tests used previously for reading and math. Based on discussions with FDOE officials and other experts, it does not appear that any such changes occurred in the years immediately before the original rating system when into effect. Therefore, the real gains in achievement from A+ may be smaller than they appear.

A third and related issue is that the more recent data provided by the FDOE for the A+ program evaluations is based on raw scores, whereas the older data used here is necessarily reported in terms of "percentages above a set standard." Unfortunately, raw scores and percentages have different statistical properties. This assumption could prove problematic, especially if the "shape of the distribution" of student ability is different across schools. In other words, the test score average across schools can differ, but the variation around that average cannot. This study tests for possible problems using the A+ data, which includes both raw scores and percentages. The use of these two measures does not significantly affect the results, as discussed later.

A fourth possible issue is that this analysis uses data for the years 1996-97 and 1997-98. The A+ ratings were released in 1999 based on data from the spring of that year. Greene then compares this with the following year's scores. Programs tend to have their biggest impacts in the early years when they receive the most attention. Therefore, it would be beneficial to analyze Florida's pre-voucher rating system using data from 1994-95 and 1995-96 to coincide with that program's first year. However, data for earlier years were not available. It is likely that the effects from pre-voucher ratings would be larger if the earlier data were used in the analysis.

A final issue is that the school rating system changed with the A+ program. Schools were still placed in categories, but the A+ ratings were based on higher standards than previously. This change could make the voucher effect look smaller, since the difficulty of further gains increases as students reach higher levels. For example, moving from the 20th percentile to the 30th percentile is likely to be easier than moving from the 30th to the 40th. The changes in tests and standards shifted 76 schools into the "F" (critically low) category that otherwise would have been in the "D" (level 2) category had the standards remained unchanged. These schools had already made large gains due to the pre-voucher ratings, discussed below.[21]

Results

Table A-1 indicates the gains by school rating and subject area for both the pre-voucher ratings and the A+ program. All of the analysis presented here is based on elementary school scores. The main reason for this restriction is that only one school was rated "critically low" at either the middle or high school level.

Schools not rated critically low were put into three higher categories, 2, 3, and 4. This rating system includes one fewer category than the A+ system. Therefore, to simplify the analysis, the A and B schools were combined into one group. This grouping will not affect the conclusions, since the focus of the analysis is on the low-scoring schools, not A and B schools. All numbers in this table, and throughout this appendix, are gain scores divided by the standard deviation, producing "effect sizes."[22]

Based on Table A-1 alone, it would appear that the A+ program is more effective than the pre-voucher grading system. However, this is quite misleading. Gains in test scores can be separated into three categories: (1) statistical "noise," e.g., a construction project going on near the testing site, which distracts students; (2) the average gain made by everyone, i.e., "trends," which may occur due to idiosyncrasies in the test and other factors; and (3) the unique gains of individual schools due to their own efforts, which are perhaps influenced by incentives created by state policy. The goal of the analysis is to separate the unique gains from statistical noise and trends. One way to account for

TABLE A-1 A simple comparison between the pre-voucher ratings and the A+ program (effect size)

	Harris: Florida ratings (1997-98)			Greene: Florida A+ (1999-2000)		
	Reading	Math	Writing	Reading	Math	Writing
All	-0.001 (1,486)	-0.007 (1,486)	-0.008 (1,486)	0.083 (2,486)	0.178 (2,486)	0.538 (2,486)
4 (A+B)	-0.013 (793)	-0.021 (793)	-0.085 (793)	0.052 (510)	0.143 (510)	0.473 (510)
3 (C)	0.007 (535)	0.006 (535)	0.080 (535)	0.066 (1,223)	0.169 (1,223)	0.529 (1,223)
2 (D)	0.035 (132)	0.019 (132)	0.097 (132)	0.143 (583)	0.229 (583)	0.612 (583)
1 (F)	0.045 (28)	0.374 (28)	0.198 (28)	0.251 (76)	0.367 (76)	1.024 (76)

Source: Author's analysis.

TABLE A-2 Adjusting gains for trends: the grand means (effect size)

	Harris: Florida ratings (1997-98)			Greene: Florida A+ (1999-2000)		
	Reading	Math	Writing	Reading	Math	Writing
4 (A+B)	-0.012	-0.014	-0.077	-0.031	-0.035	-0.065
3 (C)	0.006	0.013	0.088	-0.017	-0.009	-0.009
2 (D)	0.034	0.026	0.105	0.060	0.051	0.074
1 (F)	0.044	0.381	0.206	0.158	0.189	0.486

Source: Author's analysis.

trends is to subtract the sample mean (shown in the first row of Table A-1) from the four individual gains, shown by rating. This yields the "grand means" in **Table A-2**.

The results in Table A-2 imply a quite different conclusion. The gains in math, for instance, are now nearly twice as large in the pre-voucher ratings for the F schools (0.381 versus 0.189). However, more adjustments are necessary. The second source of variation, statistical noise, causes regression to the mean. Greene attempts to deal with this by comparing the low-scoring D schools with the high-scoring F schools. **Table A-3** includes this comparison.[23]

If this were the correct adjustment, the results would be ambiguous. The gains in math are considerably larger in the pre-voucher ratings compared with

TABLE A-3 Adjusting for regression to the mean, Greene's approach (effect size)

	Harris: Florida ratings (1997-98)			Greene: Florida A+ (1999-2000)		
	Reading	Math	Writing	Reading	Math	Writing
Low 2 (D)	0.097	0.142	0.817	0.184	0.259	0.694
High 1 (F)	0.053	0.374	0.856	0.222	0.346	0.882
Difference	-0.044	+0.132	+0.039	+0.038	+0.087	+0.186

Source: Author's analysis.

TABLE A-4 Adjusting for regression to the mean, Camilli and Bulkley approach

	Harris: Florida grading			Greene: Florida A+		
	Reading	Math	Writing	Reading	Math	Writing
4 (A+B)	+0.012	+0.023	+0.041	+0.029	+0.005	NA
3 (C)	- 0.009	- 0.026	- 0.041	-0.001	- 0.000	NA
2 (D)	- 0.031	- 0.082	- 0.151	-0.001	- 0.025	NA
1 (F)	- 0.040	+0.199	- 0.091	+0.021	+0.062	NA

Source: Author's analysis.

the A+ ratings. For writing and reading, the gains are larger for A+. However, the ongoing discussion among researchers since Greene's first paper seems to have produced agreement, even by Greene, that this is not the right approach. The standard approach in education statistics is used by Camilli and Bulkley, in which the gain scores are obtained by subtracting the second year score from the expected second year score. The expected score comes from a regression of the second year score on the first year score. Greene does not report these results in either his original paper or his response. Camilli and Bulkey do report these results, which are presented on the right hand side of **Table A-4**.

Greene is critical of this approach because *larger* real gains due to the program will, paradoxically, make the effect look *smaller*. Therefore, he suggests excluding the F schools from the regression. In theory, he is correct. However, it is highly unlikely that dropping 76 observations out of a total of 2,400 would have any meaningful impact on the results. This is confirmed by performing the same analysis as above but dropping the critically low schools from the regression. Only one of the effect sizes changes by more than 10% in any direction. Most of them changed by less than 5%, as expected.

All of the new analysis above for the pre-voucher ratings is based on the percentage of students above the 50th percentile in math and reading and the percentage achieving a 3 in writing. This method is different than Greene's analysis based on raw scores. To see whether this difference has any impact on the results, the percentages were converted into raw scores using data from 1999-2000, which include both percentages and raw scores. Specifically, it is assumed that the statistical relationship between the raw scores and the percentages remained roughly the same over the five-year period, which is likely.[24] After creating the estimated raw scores for the earlier years, the results in Table A-4 were re-estimated for reading. The results were similar, implying that the use of percentages does not significantly affect the results.

Conclusion

Based on all of the results above, it does not appear that vouchers have a significant positive impact on public school performance. Using Greene's own approach,[25] the average effect size across subjects (excluding writing) for the pre-voucher ratings is 0.08 standard deviations, compared with 0.10 for the A+ program. This means that *the real effect size of vouchers is only 0.02 standard deviations, which is quite small even by Greene's own standards*. There is still some uncertainty about these numbers, due to the factors mentioned earlier. Two of these factors indicate that the real effect is even smaller than 0.02; only one factor indicates that it is larger. Given this, it is fairly clear that the effects are small, and considerably lower than Greene's original estimates.

These results should not be surprising to those familiar with how schools work. Outside incentives may be effective, but there is no reason to believe that vouchers, based on a theory of market competition, will work better than school grades or other approaches. Regardless, tens of thousands of students remain at a major disadvantage because they attend "critically low" schools. Finding incentives that improve these schools remains an important task.

APPENDIX B

A replication of Jay Greene's voucher effect study using Texas performance data

by Amanda Brownson, Charles A. Dana Center, The University of Texas at Austin

In an article published in February 2001 by the Manhattan Institute, Jay Greene (2001) examined growth in student performance in Florida schools using achievement test scores from 1999 to 2000. The purpose of the investigation was to determine whether the accountability system, coupled with sanctions in the form of vouchers enabling students to leave schools that received an F-rating for two consecutive years, is having an effect on student performance. Specifically, Greene investigated the effect of vouchers on student performance in schools that received a state-assigned rating of F, which is their lowest of five accountability ratings, to discover whether the potential for losing students who would take their vouchers to other schools resulted in improved test scores.[26]

Greene found that campuses with an accountability rating of F improved at a faster rate than the higher-rated campuses in the state. From this analysis, he hypothesized that the threat of vouchers, which he says affect F-rated schools more than others, is the cause for this faster improvement. However, there a number of other possible explanations for this improvement unrelated to the threat of vouchers. Regression to the mean, which is the idea that extreme scores are likely to move to the average on subsequent measurements, has been discussed by Camilli and Bulkley as a possible explanation for this improvement.[27]

Purpose

A replication of Greene's analysis using data from Texas schools can shed light on this question. Texas, like Florida, administers statewide assessments and bases state-assigned accountability ratings on those assessments. In Texas, ratings range from "exemplary" to "low performing." These ratings have been assigned since 1993 and are based largely on student performance on the state's criterion-referenced test, the Texas Assessment of Academic Skills (TAAS).[28] However, Texas has not adopted a voucher policy.[29] Therefore, similar improvement in the "low-performing" schools in Texas cannot be attributed to a voucher threat.

This analysis uses a measure of student performance on TAAS called the Texas Learning Index (TLI).[30] The TLI scores were aggregated across grade levels for each campus in the state of Texas.[31] Data came from the Texas Education Agency's Academic Excellence Indicator System (AEIS) database and included all students who took the test.

FIGURE B-1 Percentage of Texas students passing all sections of the TAAS, 1994-2000

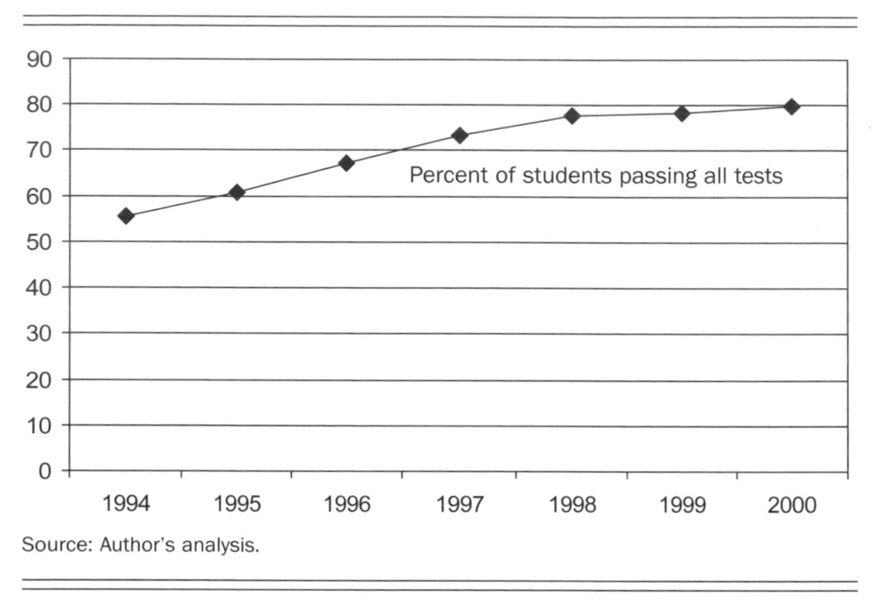

Source: Author's analysis.

This analysis replicates Greene's using data from two different two-year time periods. The first analysis uses data on student performance growth from the two-year period from 1999 to 2000. Growth from 1996 to 1997 is examined as well, because the accountability system in Texas has been in place longer than in Florida—the current version of Florida's system began in 1998. A quick look at overall Texas achievement scores in **Figure B-1** indicates that test scores were improving at a faster rate in the earlier years of TAAS administration than they are currently. The leveling off of the growth rate in Texas may indicate that it is now more difficult to demonstrate large gains. As a result, the 1996-97 data may more accurately reflect the current situation in Florida.

Finally, this analysis uses an approach described by Camilli and Bulkley in which second-year scores are regressed on first in order to compute an expected score, and then campus ratings are regressed on the difference between the expected scores and the actual second year scores.

TAAS improvement by accountability ratings

An examination of the Texas data reveals many of the same patterns that Greene found in Florida, despite the absence of a voucher threat in Texas. **Table B-1** indicates gains in reading and math test performance between the 1998-99 school year and the 1999-2000 school year aggregated at the campus level and measured by the TLI. These results are presented in standard deviations of the 1998-99 TLI scores.[32] A statistical test of mean differences was conducted to deter-

TABLE B-1 Mean differences in the Texas Learning Index between 1999 and 2000

	Mean difference (2000-1999)		
Performance category	Reading effect	Math effect	Number
Exemplary	0.011	0.066	1,094
Recognized	0.040	0.099	1,781
Acceptable	0.138	0.218	2,982
Low performing	0.456	0.773	78

Source: Author's analysis.

TABLE B-2 Mean differences in the Texas Learning Index between 1996 and 1997

	Mean difference (1997-1996)		
Performance category	Reading effect	Math effect	Number
Exemplary	0.062	0.085	385
Recognized	0.163	0.245	1,268
Acceptable	0.356	0.490	3,931
Low performing	0.771	1.2	99

Source: Author's analysis.

mine if the differences on the change variable were statistically significant between campuses within each rating category.

As was true in Florida, schools with lower ratings had larger gains between 1999 and 2000 than did schools with higher ratings. In Texas, low-performing schools demonstrated gains in both reading and math that were more than three times as high as the gains for schools with a rating of "acceptable." Tests for statistical significance on the reading exam revealed that there were statistically significant differences ($p<.05$) in the average change in TLI between all groups, except between "exemplary" and "recognized" campuses. There were statistically significant differences ($p<.05$) between all campus performance groups in math.

The 1996 to 1997 data (**Table B-2**) reveal similar patterns, though with larger gains for all groups.[33] Again, the low-performing campuses gained almost three times as much as the acceptable campuses during the same period, and this time there were statistically significant differences ($p<.01$) between all performance groups on both tests.

TABLE B-3 Isolating the effect of a low-performance rating using average TLI gains between 1999 and 2000

	Gains in reading	Number	Gains math	Number
Lower half of acceptable	0.213	1338	0.338	560
Upper half of low performing	0.231	45	0.608	62
Low-performance effect	0.018		0.274	
The Florida voucher effect	0.12		0.30	

Source: Author's analysis.

TABLE B-4 Isolating the effect of a low-performance rating using average TLI gains between 1996 and 1997

	Gains in reading	Number	Gains math	Number
Lower half of acceptable	0.456	1714	0.628	1750
Upper half of low performing	0.570	55	0.871	55
Low-performance effect	0.115		0.243	
The Florida voucher effect measured in standard deviations	0.120		0.30	

Source: Author's analysis.

Isolating a 'low-performance' effect

Greene attempted to isolate a "voucher effect" by comparing the higher-performing F schools to the lower-performing D schools. He defined higher-performing F schools as those that had average achievement that was above the mean for F schools, and lower-performing D schools as those that had average achievement below the mean for D schools. In an effort to replicate that analysis, higher-performing campuses rated low performing were compared to lower-performing campuses rated acceptable. This analysis was repeated on Texas data to see if low-performing campuses in Texas produced comparable gains without the threat of vouchers. Results reveal that the upper half of the distribution of campuses rated low performing grew at a faster rate than did the acceptable campuses in the bottom half of the distribution. **Table B-3** shows the growth of both lower-scoring acceptable campuses and higher-scoring low-performing campuses in Texas. Again, all growth is reported in standard deviations of 1999 scores for both the Texas data and the Florida data that Greene reports.

For these years, the Florida effects appear larger, with F-rated schools showing a growth of 0.12 standard deviations in math compared to 0.018 for

Texas, and growth of 0.3 in reading compared to 0.184 for Texas. In both Florida and Texas, the difference was significant for the math test, and not for the reading test.

A replication of this process using gains from 1996 to 1997 shows similar differences, and the Texas low-performance effect now appears to be comparable to the effect that Greene found in Florida. **Table B-4** compares the growth of low-scoring acceptable campuses and higher-scoring low-performing campuses for the 1996 to 1997 data.

For data from 1996 to 1997, the differences between the higher-performing low-performing campuses and the lower-performing acceptable campuses was statistically significant ($p<.05$) for both reading and math gains.

Greene used a second approach to account for possible regression to the mean. He regressed change scores on higher-scoring F and lower-scoring F schools, holding constant prior achievement scores. He argued that if the improvements for the lower-scoring F schools were not a great deal larger than for the higher-scoring F schools, one can safely rule out regression to the mean as the cause of the improvement in F schools and attribute it to a voucher threat. He found that both halves of the distribution of F-rated schools showed statistically significant effects and argued that regression to the mean was not the cause for this effect because the higher-scoring F schools had either larger or similar effects as the lower-scoring F-schools.

A replication of this analysis using Texas data from 1999 to 2000 indicated that, for reading, much of the improvement in the low-performing category may be due to regression to the mean. The lower half of the distribution of low-performing schools had a larger effect than the upper half of the low-performing campuses. Gains in the upper half of the low-performing campus group did not achieve statistical significance.

However, the upper half of the low-performing campus group did show statistically significant effects on the math exam, although the coefficient for the upper half was smaller than the lower half. This may indicate that, while regression to the mean accounts for some of the low-performance effect in math, there may be some other explanation as well. **Table B-5** shows the regression results for the upper half and lower half of low-performing campuses using the 1999 to 2000 data.

A replication of these analyses using 1996 and 1997 data indicate stronger evidence of a low-performance effect. For these years, both the higher and lower halves of the distribution of low-performing campuses showed statistically significant performance gains for both tests. **Table B-6** shows the regression results for the upper and lower halves of the low-performing campuses using the 1996 to 1997 data.

Camilli and Bulkley (2001) propose a different method for correcting for regression to the mean. In this approach, the difference between actual and expected scores is regressed on campus ratings, and, in Texas, low-performing

Table B-5 Regression of TLI change on low performance, 1999-2000

	Reading effect	P value	Math effect	P value
Constant	2.329	.000	2.966	.000
Prior performance	-0.027	.000	-0.040	.000
Upper half of low performing	0.018	.816	0.157	.007
Lower half of low performing	0.235	.012	0.614	.000

Source: Author's analysis.

Table B-6 Regression of TLI change on low performance, 1996-97

	Reading effect	P value	Math effect	P value
Constant	2.555	.000	3.336	.000
Prior performance	-0.028	.000	-0.038	.000
Upper half of low performing	0.243	.000	0.274	.000
Lower half of low performing	0.367	.000	0.644	.000

Source: Author's analysis.

schools gain more ground than do schools with other ratings for both exams and during both time periods; consistent with the other tests, the effect in math is larger than in reading.

As shown in **Table B-7**, for the 1999 to 2000 data, all campus ratings show statistical significance, and low-performing campuses show stronger gains than other campuses on both tests, but especially in math. Interestingly, acceptable campuses actually seem to lose some ground once the effect of regression to the mean is removed.

As indicated in **Table B-8**, for the 1996 to 1997 data there is a much more practically significant effect for low-performing campuses, which show growth of almost half of a standard deviation in math.

Summary

The above results indicate that schools rated low performing in Texas do grow at a faster rate than other schools even without the threat of vouchers, casting doubt on Greene's claim that a voucher threat was the impetus for such growth in Florida. Low-performing schools in Texas show stronger growth rates than other campuses both when using a replication of the method that Greene used and when employing a different and more commonly used correction for regression to the mean. Furthermore, when using data from 1996 to 1997, which

Table B-7 School rating effects correcting for regression to the mean, 1999 to 2000

Campus rating	Reading effect	P value	Math effect	P value
Exemplary	.125	.000	.111	.000
Recognized	.066	.000	.053	.000
Acceptable	-.042	.000	.037	.000
Low performing	.145	.016	.274	.000

Source: Author's analysis.

Table B-8 School rating effects correcting for regression to the mean, 1996 to 1997

Campus rating	Reading effect	P value	Math effect	P value
Exemplary	-.033	.181	-.039	.138
Recognized	-.038	.012	-.020	.214
Acceptable	.006	.435	.000	.997
Low performing	.280	.000	.404	.000

Source: Author's analysis.

probably more accurately reflect the current climate in Florida, the effects for low-performing campuses in Texas show gains that appear comparable to the F-rated campuses in Florida.

APPENDIX C

A replication of Jay Greene's voucher effect study using North Carolina data

by Helen F. Ladd and Elizabeth J. Glennie, Sanford Institute of Public Policy, Duke University

Jay Greene of the Manhattan Institute has recently used the large gains in student test scores in Florida's lowest-performing schools to argue that the threat of a voucher leads to school improvement. Because the lowest-performing schools (those rated F in Florida) are the only ones subject to the threat of a voucher, he attributes the larger achievement gains in those schools compared to the gains in the schools rated D to fear of the voucher program. He then refined the approach by comparing the gains in the top half of the F group of schools to those in the bottom half of the D group.

We believe that Greene has inappropriately attributed the differential gains to the voucher program rather than to the other effects of being labeled a failing school, such as shame, increased scrutiny, and possibly additional resources. To provide evidence to support this interpretation, we have replicated his study as closely as possible for North Carolina, a state that rates schools but does not have a voucher program. The logic of our approach is identical to his. The analysis differs only in that the North Carolina ABC's accountability program uses a somewhat different rating system. We base our analysis on test scores in math and reading in grades 3-8 and writing where appropriate.

In North Carolina, the four main categories of schools are exemplary, meets expectations, no recognition and low performing. We view the low-performing schools as comparable to Florida's F-rated schools. In contrast to Florida, North Carolina puts much more emphasis on the gains in scores from one year to the next in ranking the schools. In fact, it is the size of the gains relative to expected gains that essentially determine the top three categories. Each school's expected gain is based on predicted statewide gains by subject and grade level, with small and partially offsetting adjustments for regression to the mean and the initial proficiency of the students.

Exemplary schools meet their expected gains in test scores by more than 10%, and schools meeting expectations are those that have gains at least as large as the gains expected for them. No-recognition schools exhibit gains in student performance below their expected gains. Finally, low-performing schools meet neither a growth nor a performance standard. Such schools do not meet their expected growth and the percent of students at grade level falls short of the 50% performance standard.

TABLE C-1A Changes in performance composite, North Carolina, 1997-98

1997 school evaluation	Average difference in composite	Number of schools
Exemplary	2.37	514
Expected growth	3.43	380
No recognition	4.94	551
Low performing	10.68	114

The change for low-performing schools compared to schools with higher evaluations is statistically significant at $p<.0001$.

TABLE C-1B Changes in growth composite, North Carolina, 1997-98

1997 school evaluation	Average difference in composite	Number of schools
Exemplary	2.11	514
Expected growth	4.66	380
No recognition	7.48	551
Low performing	10.98	114

The change for low-performing schools compared to schools with higher evaluations is statistically significant at $p<.0001$.

Source: Authors' analysis.

Method and results

Relying on publicly available data, we first grouped schools by the classification they received from the state in 1997 (exemplary growth, expected growth, no recognition, low performing) and examined two different measures of changes in student performance from 1997 (the first year of the ABCs accountability program) to 1998: the change in the performance composite and the change in the growth composite. The performance composite is the percent of students at or above grade level in each year based on reading, math, and writing scores. The growth composite is the gain in test scores minus the expected gain in test scores in each year. Thus, the change in the performance composite is a change in levels, namely the change in the percent of the students scoring at grade level or above from one year to the next. The change in the growth composite is the difference between the gains in test scores relative to expected gains during the 1997-98 school year and the 1996-97 school year.

For both measures of change, low-performing schools had a greater positive change than any other school type, and significance tests of the difference

TABLE C-2A Changes in performance composite, North Carolina, 1997-98, comparing 'most similar' schools

1997 school evaluation	Average difference in composite	Number of schools
Lower-scoring no recognition	5.91	272
Higher-scoring low performing	9.22	57

The difference between the gains for the two school types is statistically significant at p<.0001.

TABLE C-2B Changes in growth composite, North Carolina, 1997-98, comparing 'most similar' schools

1997 school evaluation	Average difference in composite	Number of schools
Lower-scoring no recognition	7.24	272
Higher-scoring low performing	9.46	57

The difference between the gains for the two school types is statistically significant at p<.0001.

Source: Authors' analysis.

between the change for low-performing schools and that of every other school type show that these differences are statistically significant. In other words, the gains in student achievement observed in the low-performing schools differed from those in other schools by an amount that is very unlikely to have been produced by chance alone (see **Table C-1**.)

Following Greene's logic that high-performing F schools in Florida are very much like low-performing D schools in terms of incentives to improve their performance and challenges in doing so, we compared the high-scoring low-performing schools in North Carolina to low-scoring no-recognition schools. High-scoring low-performing schools are those in the top half of the 1997 performance composite score range, and low-scoring no-recognition schools are those in the bottom half of the 1997 performance composite score range. Repeating the above analysis for this subset of schools shows the same result: high-scoring low-performance schools had a higher gain did than low-scoring no-recognition schools, and this difference is statistically significant. This is true both for comparisons of gains in performance composite and growth composite. (See **Table C-2**.)

Conclusion

We conclude from this North Carolina analysis that the results that Jay Greene found for Florida probably have little or nothing to do with vouchers. If vouchers were the explanation for the gains in the F-rated schools in Florida, it is unlikely we would have found comparable patterns of gains in the low-performing schools in North Carolina.

Endnotes

1. In his latest book, *The Black-White Test Score Gap* (co-edited with Meredith Phillips, 1998), Jencks seems to argue that the biggest cause of the persistent gap is differences in family characteristics over which schools, public or private, have very little control. But he does suggest that some school improvements, like smaller classes or better-prepared teachers, might make a difference.

2. By the fourth year of the program, there were only 40 children left in the unsuccessful applicant comparison group, making their average test score highly sensitive to either high or low scores (Witte 1997).

3. Only 8,000 pupils had taken vouchers by the year 2000. Private schools not in operation when vouchers were offered had to be approved, limiting the supply of new schools. About 90 private schools, 80% religious, took voucher students in 2000-01. According to recent applications, 22 new private schools, still mainly religious, should be approved in 2001-02, enrolling another 2,000 children. Even so, the supply of schools to take advantage of a fairly large voucher ($5,300) is slow in materializing.

4. Many of the children receiving vouchers were scheduled to enter kindergarten in 1995, just as Cleveland abolished full-day kindergarten. This change could have influenced parents to take vouchers.

5. Between year 1 and year 2, 26 third graders in non-Hope Schools did not return to the program (approximately 20%). These were students who achieved significantly lower than other voucher students in the third grade even though all had statistically similar second-grade test results. All left the Cleveland school district.

6. This tuition arrangement differs from the Milwaukee experiment. Private schools in Milwaukee were not allowed to charge tuition over and above the voucher.

7. A 0.10 level of statistical significance indicates that there is a 20% probability that the gain reported is not different from zero. The reporting standard in such studies considers this to be a relatively "high" chance that the gain is indeed not different from zero.

8. These calculations use simple arithmetic means of test score gains for the three cities weighted by the number of observations in each year in each city. The Peterson group paper estimated averages using more complex weights, but it did not provide the data that would have enabled others to test or replicate the conclusions. However, the differences between the averages in Figure B and averages using the Peterson group's weights would be small.

9. Many of the students who applied for vouchers and who were initially tested were already attending private schools (up to 45% in Dayton). Up to one-third (again, in Dayton) of voucher recipients were also already attending private schools. However, the results in all the cities are reported only for those students initially in public school.

10. We would *not* expect a similar effect for children assigned to normal classes in the Tennessee experiment because there both satisfied and dissatisfied parents participated in the random draw.

11. In effect, this turns out to be similar to dividing the unbiased estimate of receiving a voucher by the probability of using the voucher. For example, the estimated reading gain for black students of receiving a voucher was 3.5 percentiles, and the gain of switching to a private school 6.1 percentiles. The ratio of 3.5 to 6.1 is 57%, approximately the probability of voucher recipients actually using the voucher.

12. In fact, the higher-scoring F schools had slightly higher average test scores from the previous year than lower-scoring D schools. This outcome can result because the state grade assigned to schools depends on the percentage of students above a certain threshold on the test score, not by the average test score for the school.

13. As Camilli and Bulkley note (in their footnote 2), this is specified under Rule 6A-1.09981 of the State Board of Education Administrative Rules.

14. In this first round of analyses, Browson does not make the overall correction for regression to the mean because she is trying to make a direct comparison to Greene's results.

15. In duplicating Greene's analysis, Brownson used the same assumptions he made regarding regression-to-the-mean effects. When she re-estimates the relative gains for failing schools in Texas using the Camilli-Bulkley method rather than the Greene method of comparing high-performing F schools to low-performing D schools, the relative gains to F schools increase for reading in both 1999-2000 and 1996-97, and for math in 1996-97.

16. According to Ladd, "[E]xemplary schools meet their expected gains in test scores by more than 10 percent and schools meeting expectations are those that have gains at least as large as the gains expected for them. No recognition schools exhibit gains in student performance below their expected gains. Finally, low-performing schools meet neither a growth nor a performance standard. Such schools do not meet their expected growth and the percent of students at grade level falls short of the 50 percent performance standard."

17. Hoxby's characterization of randomized field trials appears in Howell et al. 2000b, p. 2.

18. Good school management can also run out quickly, particularly since, as private schools expand in inner cities, they face the same fundamental problems as do public schools (see Leovy 2000).

19. One problem with this recent analysis, by Howell and Peterson, however, is that most of the positive result for African Americans in New York City is located in the single fifth/sixth-grade cohort. There might exist a particular cohort effect in that group that has little to do with private schools attended. The fifth/sixth-grade cohort of African Americans is a small proportion of the total African American sample. The difference in test scores between the rest of the African American sample attending private schools and Latinos attending private schools is probably very low to start with, so explaining an already small difference in test scores with school variable differences is unlikely to produce significant results.

20. The authors thank officials at the Florida Department of Education for this and other useful information.

21. According to documentation obtained from the Florida State Board of Education, the original low rating was given when, for two consecutive years, fewer than 33% of students had scored above the 50th percentile on reading and math, and fewer than 33% scored 3 or above on the Florida state writing test. As stated earlier, the newer standards are more stringent, but are difficult to compare because the testing instrument changed.

22. Different standard deviations are required for the 1995-97 data compared with the

1998-2000 data. In the latter case, the sample standard deviations calculated by Camilli and Bulkley are used. In the former case, it is assumed that the relationship between the cross-school standard deviation and the cross-student standard deviation is similar to that calculated by Camilli and Bulkley. Specifically, they found that the cross-student variation is 3.5 times larger in math and reading and 2.2 times larger in writing.

23. All of the regression-to-the-mean adjustments made throughout this appendix automatically adjust for trends; therefore, no additional corrections are necessary to find the real effects.

24. This was accomplished by regressing the raw scores on the percentages. The independent variables included percentages, percentages squared, and percentages cubed. The estimated equation was then applied to the data for earlier years.

25. Greene used two approaches. The one used here is the one he used in his response, subtracting the second-year score from the expected value of the second-year score, based on a regression that excludes the F schools.

26. Florida assigns campus ratings A through F based primarily on the Florida Comprehensive Assessment Test (FCAT).

27. It may also be that the publication of a low accountability rating by itself, or in conjunction with other sanctions besides vouchers, could cause such improvement.

28. See the Texas Accountability Manual at http://www.tea.state.tx.us/perfreport/account/2000/manual/ for a description of the Texas system.

29. While vouchers are not available to Texas families, the option of attending a public charter school does exist. In 1997-98, Texas had 19 charter schools. In the 1999-2000 school year, Texas had 160 charter schools serving about 35,000 students (roughly 0.7% of Texas public school enrollment). In most areas of the state, public charter schools do not offer a meaningful alternative to parents of students attending low-performing schools. First, there are relatively few charter schools from which to choose (they represent 2% of Texas public school campuses). In addition, the distinctive nature of charter schools (over half have programs specifically designed to serve students at risk of school failure and dropout) means that they are not appropriate for the typical student. Most important, student performance in Texas public charter schools is disappointingly low. In 2000, 11.4% of charter schools were rated low performing, compared with 2.1% of traditional public schools rated low performing. Another 13% of the public charter schools were rated "needs peer review"—an indication that the school has other difficulties.

30. For a description of the Texas Learning Index, see the *Technical Digest,* which can be found online at http://www.tea.state.tx.us/student.assessment/resources/techdig/index.html.

31. Camilli and Bulkley (2001) argue that aggregation across grade levels is inappropriate because diagnostic information regarding different effects in different grades may be lost, and because scales of different instruments should not be combined. This analysis aggregates across grade levels in order to replicate Greene's analysis as closely as possible, in spite of some possible limitations.

32. The standard deviation for the average reading TLI in 1999 was 6.6647. The standard deviation of the average math TLI was 6.3705

33. The standard deviation for the average reading TLI in 1996 was 5.61. The standard deviation of the average math TLI in 1996 was 5.36.

References

American Federation of Teachers (AFT). 1997. "Miracle or Mirage? Behind the Cleveland Hope Schools Voucher Students Study." Washington, D.C.: AFT.

Camilli, Gregory, and Katrina Bulkley. 2001. "Critique of an 'Evaluation of the Florida A-Plus Accountability and School Choice Program." *Educational Policy Analysis Archives* 9(7), March 4. <http://epaa.asu.edu/v9n7/>

Friedman, Milton. 1955. "The Role of Government in Education." In Robert Solo, ed., *Economics and the Public Interest*. New Brunswick, N.J.: Rutgers University Press.

Greene, Jay P. 2000. "The Effect of School Choice: An Evaluation of the Charlotte Children's Scholarship Fund." Civic Report No. 12. New York, N.Y.: Manhattan Institute for Policy Research, Center for Civic Innovation.

Greene, Jay. 2001. "An Evaluation of the Florida A-Plus Accountability and School Choice Program." New York, N.Y.: Manhattan Institute for Policy Research, Center for Civic Innovation. <http://www.manhattan-institute.org/html/cr_aplus.htm>

Greene, Jay. 2001. "A Reply to 'Critique of an "Evaluation of the Florida A-Plus Accountability and School Choice Program,"' by Gregory Camilli and Katrina Bulkley." New York, N.Y.: Manhattan Institute for Policy Research.

Greene, Jay P., William G. Howell, and Paul E. Peterson. 1998. "Lessons From the Cleveland Scholarship Program." In Paul E. Peterson and Bryan C. Hassel, eds., *Learning From School Choice.* Washington, D.C.: Brookings Institution.

Greene, Jay P., Paul E. Peterson, and Jiangtao Du. 1996. "The Effectiveness of School Choice in Milwaukee: A Secondary Analysis of Data From the Program's Evaluation." Paper prepared for the Panel on the Political Analysis of Urban School Systems, American Political Science Association, San Francisco, Calif., August 30.

Howell, William, Patrick Wolf, Paul Peterson, and David Campbell. 2000a. "Test Score Effects of School Vouchers in Dayton, Ohio, New York City, and Washington, D.C.: Evidence From Randomized Field Trials." Paper prepared for the American Political Science Association meeting, September.

Howell, William, Patrick Wolf, Paul Peterson, and David Campbell. 2000b. "The Effect of School Vouchers on Student Achievement: A Response to Critics." Cambridge, Mass.: Harvard Program on Educational Policy and Governance. <ksg.harvard.edu/pepg/>

Jencks, Christopher. 1966. "Is the Public School Obsolete?" *The Public Interest* 2, Winter, 18-27.

Jencks, Christopher, and Meredith Phillips, eds. 1998. *The Black-White Test Score Gap.* Washington, D.C.: Brookings Institution Press.

Kupermintz, Haggai. 2001. "The Effects of Vouchers on School Improvement: Another Look at the Florida Data." *Educational Policy Analysis Archives* 9(8), March 9. <http://epaa.asu.edu/v9n8/>

Leovy, Jill. 2000. "School Voucher Program Teaches Hard Lessons." *Los Angeles Times,* October 9.

Metcalf, Kim K., et. al. 1998. "Evaluation of the Cleveland Scholarship Program: Second Year Report." Bloomington: Indiana Center for Evaluation, Indiana University.

Metcalf, Kim K., et al. 1999. "Evaluation of the Cleveland Scholarship and Tutoring Grant Program, 1996-1999." Bloomington: Indiana Center for Evaluation, Indiana University.

Mosteller, Frederick. 1995. *The Tennessee Study of Class Size in the Early School Grades.* Somerville, Mass.: American Academy of Arts and Sciences.

Peterson, Paul E., Jay P. Greene, and William G. Howell. 1998. "New Findings for the Cleveland Scholarship Program: A Reanalysis of Data From the Indiana University School of Education Evaluation." Cambridge, Mass.: Harvard University Program in Education Policy and Governance. Mimeo.

Peterson, Paul E., William G. Howell, and Jay P. Greene. 1999. "An Evaluation of the Cleveland Voucher Program After Two Years." Cambridge, Mass.: Harvard University Program in Education Policy and Governance. Mimeo.

Peterson, Paul E., and William Howell. 2001. "Exploring Explanations for Ethnic Differences in Voucher Impacts on Student Test Scores." Paper presented at a conference cosponsored by the Brookings Institution and Edison Schools, "Closing the Gap: Promising Approaches to Reducing the Achievement Gap," February 1-2.

Reich, Robert B. 2000. "The Case for 'Progressive' Vouchers." *Wall Street Journal*, September 6.

Rouse, Cecilia. 1998a. "Private School Vouchers and Student Achievement: Evidence From the Milwaukee Choice Program." *Quarterly Journal of Economics*, 113(2): 553-602.

Rouse, Cecilia. 1998b. "Schools and Student Achievement: More Evidence From the Milwaukee Parental Choice Program." *Federal Reserve Bank of New York Economic Policy Review*, 4(1):61-76. <www.ny.frb.org>

Safire, William. 2000. "Are School Vouchers the Answer?" *New York Times*, August 31.

Steele, Claude M., and Joshua Aronson. 1998. "Stereotype Threat and the Test Performance of Academically Successful African Americans." In Christopher Jencks and Meredith Phillips, eds., *The Black-White Test Score Gap*. Washington, D.C.: Brookings Institution Press.

Williams, Joe. 2000. "Choice May Draw 10,000 Students in Fall; 22 New Schools Will Join Voucher Program for Next School Year, DPI Announces." *Milwaukee Journal Sentinel,* May 16.

Witte, John F. 1993. "The Milwaukee Parental Choice Program." In M. Edith Rasell and Richard Rothstein, eds., *School Choice: Examining the Evidence*. Washington, D.C.: Economic Policy Institute.

Witte, John F. 1997. "Reply to Greene, Peterson and Du: 'The Effectiveness of School Choice in Milwaukee: A Secondary Analysis of Data From the Program's Evaluation.'" <http://hdc-www.harvard.edu/pepg/op/evaluate.htm>.

Witte, John F., Troy D. Sterr, and Christopher A. Thorn. 1995. "Fifth Year Report: Milwaukee Parental Choice Program." Madison, Wis.: Department of Political Science and the Robert M. La Follette Center for Public Affairs, University of Wisconsin.

About EPI

The Economic Policy Institute was founded in 1986 to widen the debate about policies to achieve healthy economic growth, prosperity, and opportunity.

Today, despite recent rapid growth in the U.S. economy, inequality in wealth, wages, and income remains historically high. Expanding global competition, changes in the nature of work, and rapid technological advances are altering economic reality. Yet many of our policies, attitudes, and institutions are based on assumptions that no longer reflect real world conditions.

With the support of leaders from labor, business, and the foundation world, the Institute has sponsored research and public discussion of a wide variety of topics: trade and fiscal policies; trends in wages, incomes, and prices; education; the causes of the productivity slowdown; labor market problems; rural and urban policies; inflation; state-level economic development strategies; comparative international economic performance; and studies of the overall health of the U.S. manufacturing sector and of specific key industries.

The Institute works with a growing network of innovative economists and other social science researchers in universities and research centers all over the country who are willing to go beyond the conventional wisdom in considering strategies for public policy.

Founding scholars of the Institute include Jeff Faux, EPI president; Lester Thurow, Sloan School of Management, MIT; Ray Marshall, former U.S. secretary of labor, professor at the LBJ School of Public Affairs, University of Texas; Barry Bluestone, University of Massachusetts-Boston; Robert Reich, former U.S. secretary of labor; and Robert Kuttner, author, editor of *The American Prospect,* and columnist for *Business Week* and the Washington Post Writers Group.

For additional information about the Institute, contact EPI at 1660 L Street NW, Suite 1200, Washington, D.C. 20036, (202) 775-8810, or visit www.epinet.org.